GEORGIAN
HOUSE STYLE

AN ARCHITECTURAL AND INTERIOR DESIGN SOURCE BOOK

GEORGIAN
HOUSE STYLE

AN ARCHITECTURAL AND INTERIOR DESIGN SOURCE BOOK
INGRID CRANFIELD

David & Charles

Contents

Preface

by Professor James Stevens Curl FSA

By 'Georgian' is meant the period 1714 to 1830 during which the Hanoverian Electors were also Kings of Great Britain and Ireland, reigning as George I, II, III, and IV. George IV was also Prince Regent during the incapacity of his father, George III, so the Georgian age embraces that period of high fashion and élan known as the Regency, much influenced by French *Empire* taste.

'Georgian' is a term usually associated in the popular mind with refined furniture, elegant clothes, buildings of deceptive simplicity, Classical music, decorous prose, and country houses set in pleasing parks. Yet there was far more to it than that. True, the first fifty years of the Georgian Age were dominated by the second Palladian Revival of which Colen Campbell (1676–1729) and Richard Boyle, Third Earl of Burlington and Fourth Earl of Cork (1694–1753), were the progenitors, and the rules of proportion and composition laid down were enshrined in the many pattern-books that provided the means by which even the untalented could produce reasonably competent designs. However, as the century progressed, the range of styles available was extended, and included Gothick (a style owing little to mediaeval precedent), Rococo, Chinoiserie, Hindoo, neo-Classicism, Greek Revival, Egyptian Revival, and much else. By the end of the Georgian period the stylistic cornucopia was flowing over, offering an enormous, even bewildering, number of choices, leading to an uninhibited gusto when it came to architecture and interior design. The brilliant eclectic vulgarity of Brighton Pavilion, for example, was anything but staid or reserved, and reflected the spirit of Regency times.

It is another popular misconception that the Industrial Revolution occurred in the reign of Queen Victoria (1837–1901), yet it and the Agrarian Revolution were phenomena of the Georgian period. Furthermore, by the middle of the eighteenth century, perception of the countryside was changing as aesthetic sensibilities became attuned to new ways of looking at things. At the beginning of the century, mountainous landscapes such as those of the Scottish Highlands and the English Lake District were regarded as frightful and dreary, while agricultural areas were of no interest at all as scenery. The Georgians began to appreciate landscapes because they had them made to look like paintings, so the Picturesque (from *pittoresco*, meaning 'in the manner of the painters') came into being. The Georgian landowner, viewing his recently created 'landskip' from his Palladian pile, saw himself as a modern Roman, a Pliny, with scenery of Virgilian loveliness surrounding his house. Often this involved the moving of whole villages, the planting of enormous numbers of trees, the creation of artificial lakes, and the making of 'naturally' undulating land where before everything was flat and dull.

Apart from the Picturesque, there were two other aesthetic categories: the Beautiful and the Sublime. The former derived from a compound ratio of uniformity and variety, according to some, while to others it was created by an association of fitness of form, shape, size, and scale for function, because proportions, openings in walls, and masses of structure looked right and gave pleasure for the simple reason that they looked as though they would actually work and remain stable. Others opined that Beauty derived from smallness, smoothness, absence of angularity or of anything that jarred, and the presence of brightness and clarity of colour. Beauty was associated with pleasure and the 'emotion of Taste'.

The third category, the Sublime, was associated with terror, wildness, splendour, darkness, vastness, and powerful, irrational emotion. Edmund Burke (1729–97), in his *A Philosophical Enquiry into the Origin of our Ideas of the Sublime and Beautiful (1756),* recognised the power of suggestiveness to stimulate the imagination, and it was with the recognition of the Sublime that wild, mountainous landscapes, severe, unadorned architecture, and the terrible grandeur of industry began to be appreciated, perhaps with a delicious shiver of apprehension, and enormous mills, canal aqueducts, railway viaducts, and cavernous warehouses might prod associations, fancy, and flights of the mind. Sensibilities began to respond to the untamed ruggedness of nature in all its *aweful* might, and rugged scenery was recognised as Sublime rather than dismissed as 'dismal' or worse.

The Georgian legacy, then, was not only a perfected system of design based on refined austerity, clarity, and logic, embracing the Beautiful, but saw the transformation of composition through the pursuit of novelty and a wide range of precedents (some of them archaeological and others exotic), a broadening of aesthetic possibilities and associations, and the acceptance of the irrational as well as the Apollonian qualities of the Age of Reason. For its exuberance, inventiveness, beauty, and essential *agreeableness*, unspoiled by moralising rhetoric or humourless cant, the Georgian period deserves our admiration and respect. Its refinement was balanced by its zest, its measured prose and poetry by rumbustious bawdy, and its reticence by stunning lushness and invention.

James Stevens Curl is Professor of Architectural History, Centre for Conservation Studies, De Montfort University, Leicester. He is the author of many books, including Georgian Architecture *(David & Charles, 1993 and 1996),* A Celebration of Death *(B.T. Batsford, 1993),* Egyptomania *(Manchester University Press, 1994), and* The English Heritage Book of Victorian Churches *(B T Batsford, 1995).*

Introduction

'Materials in Architecture are like words in Phraseology which singly have little or no power, and may be so arranged as to excite contempt yet when combined with Art, and expressed with energy, they actuate the mind with unbounded sway.'

William Chambers, 1798

England was at peace between 1713 and 1739, but the eighteenth century as a whole was a period of war and diplomacy. The American War of Independence produced as bitter a debate and ultimate defeat in England as it accorded a hard-won victory in America. The Second Treaty of Paris of 1782 recognised a new independent America south from the Great Lakes and west of the Mississippi. Industrial output soared during the 1780s, as did English exports to America, rising from a value of £12.5 million in 1782 to £20 million in 1790.

In England, land remained the principal source of wealth and power. Peers who had owned 15–20 per cent of England's landed wealth in 1700, owned 20–25 per cent by 1800. The landed gentry, below them in the social scale, were likewise able to increase their wealth as a result of improvements in agriculture, of royalties from coal and iron production, or urban development (the Bedfords and the Grosvenors were the leading landlords in London) and of the building of ports and canals. Land values nearly doubled between 1700 and 1790 as more land was brought under cultivation. The enclosure of fields continued during this period, mainly by acts of parliament, it being considered a necessary prelude to agricultural improvement since great farms were thought to effect great achievements, while small tenures would yield 'nothing but beggars and weeds'. With the advance of enclosure, the countryside changed; woodlands and waste ground gave way to new hedges, walls, fences and roads. With enclosure, rents rose

and so did farm profits, but there were those who resented the deprivation of their independence, which left them without the means to improve their lot. Many former small owner-occupiers became rural labourers or had to turn to other livelihoods; many ended as paupers, dependent on relief allowances when bad harvests led to soaring wheat prices.

All was not misery and hopelessness, however. The

desired town houses in addition to, and often in the same style as, their country homes.

Georgian house style was born in London out of a marriage between speculative wealth and taste, and a practical desire for permanence. In 1615, when Inigo Jones was appointed surveyor to James I, the City of London had many timber buildings in traditional styles, with low horizontal windows. Jones's design for the Queen's House at Greenwich (now part of the National Maritime Museum) was one of the first great initiators of change. Its plain brick front had tall, narrow windows, precursors in proportions of the sash windows that were to become characteristic of the Georgian period. The Duke of Bedford, impressed by this new style, adopted it for the construction of the Covent Garden Piazza (now nearly all destroyed), where plain brick houses were built in terraces forming a central open space on the Italian pattern. In about 1640 a row of red-brick houses in Great Queen Street nearby was built and presumably designed in a free version of Jones's style by Peter Mills, a bricklayer, complete with tall and narrow casement windows and a Classical wooden cornice at eaves level. This scheme, with continuous terraces in two rows facing each other, constituted what was, in the eighteenth century, reputed to be 'the first regular street in London'. Not only did this lay the foundation of the street, and accordingly town plan for the next two centuries and more, it also set in place a canon of design for elevations. Here was the basis of the Classicism, derived from the Ancient world, that characterised so much of Georgian building. House façades represented a Classical order as expressed in Ancient Greece and Rome in the form of a column raised on a podium: here the ground floor corresponded to the podium, the upper floors to the column, with the emphasis at first-floor level from which the main part of the order arose. At the beginning of the Georgian age, once the Baroque inheritance had grown wearisome and had been discarded, Palladianism – a return to the Classical canons of architectural design as laid down by Andrea Palladio (1508–80) and interpreted principally by Jones – became the norm of British architecture, not only at the highest levels in great public buildings but throughout the land, permeating the workshops of the most modest carpenter and bricklayer.

This time, too, witnessed the heyday of the speculative builder. London had been enlarged after the Civil War (1642–6) by the house-building of a flamboyant entrepreneur called Dr Nicholas Barbon, but by and large houses had previously been built for a specific person; now, with the growth in population and demand for housing in towns, the poorer classes clamouring for accommodation became easy prey. Initially they were given minimum housing for a trifling rent; later, with the expansion of urban life and of the professional classes, the town house, neither a mansion nor a hovel, became the standard unit of residential currency. A system of leasehold tenure promoted by

eighteenth century, according to some historians, witnessed the 'birth of the consumer society', and certainly fashion and taste became widespread preoccupations, filtering down from the élite at least as far as the provincial middle classes. Bath and Bristol and other spa towns boomed; romanticism blossomed in the arts; the Grand Tour through France, Italy and Germany became the desideratum, if not the expectation, of the well-to-do. The poor continued to be restless, however, and frequent riots occurred, particularly in London where they were aimed primarily at rich men's houses, and also in the countryside, where the many inequalities offended the common person's sense of fairness.

The Industrial Revolution, seen by some in retrospect as more of an evolution since many of the social and economic processes encouraged by it had been gathering force since a century earlier, nevertheless produced a great leap forward, with towns such as Manchester, Sheffield and York growing dramatically. The characters of the towns and their working populations differed, however, but they had many features in common, in particular working-class housing in long rows of brick terraces. The great demand for new houses now developed into a passion of construction. Landed gentry and aristocrats

OPPOSITE PAGE: *Chimneypiece bearing a relief depicting a sacrifice to Bacchus, carved by Michael Rysbrack, one of the foremost sculptors of the early eighteenth century; Clandon Park, Surrey.*

RIGHT: *The marble hall of Clandon Park, built in Classical style by the Venetian architect Giacomo Leoni c.1731 for the second Lord Onslow. The hall is a single 40ft (12.2m) cube, with two chimneypieces, each with a relief carved by Michael Rysbrack.*

hereditary landlords brought huge swaths of development into being. Under this system, plots were let at a low ground rent on the understanding that the lessee built a house or houses, at his own expense, these buildings to become, at the end of the lease, the property of the ground landlord. As leases became longer – 99 years was almost universal by the end of the seventeenth century – greater concessions were allowed the lessee, in the form of a nominal rent for the first few years while he incurred the expense of building. Some aristocratic landlords, beginning with Lord St Albans in 1665, succeeded in winning the freehold to property, which made it worthwhile for the landlord to include in his building scheme a house for himself and his family, which would be transmitted down the generations. Furthermore, it was soon realised that houses on their own could not provide a satisfactory living environment: they had to be part of a complete unit of development, comprising a square, some smaller, less expensive streets, a market and perhaps a church.

In the early seventeenth century there had been large fires in

RIGHT: *Drawing by Thomas H. Shepherd of Sussex Place, Regent's Park, London, published 5 May 1827. This was one of a series of 'views of the new and most interesting objects in the British metropolis & its vicinity'.*

OPPOSITE PAGE: *A selection of designs for balconies, which were considered essential embellishments for the first floor of larger types of houses.*

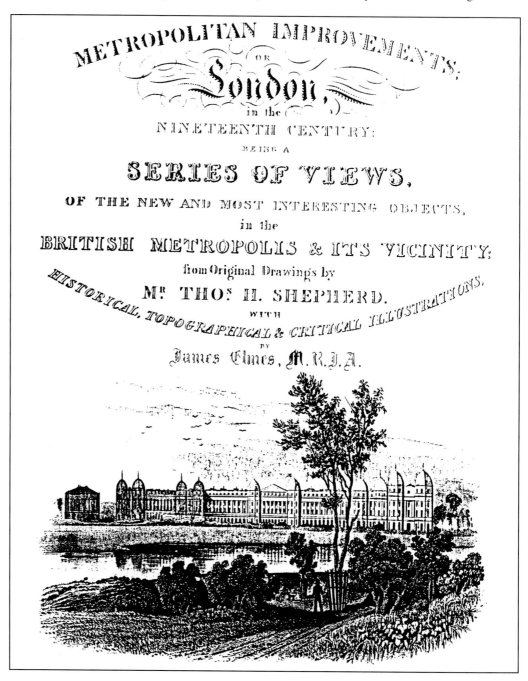

METROPOLITAN IMPROVEMENTS;
OR
London,
in the
NINETEENTH CENTURY:
BEING A
SERIES OF VIEWS,
OF THE NEW AND MOST INTERESTING OBJECTS,
in the
BRITISH METROPOLIS & ITS VICINITY:
from Original Drawings by
Mr THOS. H. SHEPHERD.
WITH
HISTORICAL, TOPOGRAPHICAL & CRITICAL ILLUSTRATIONS,
BY
James Elmes, M.R.I.A.

London and many other places, including Northampton, Marlborough and Bury St Edmunds, but it was the Great Fire of London that shifted the course of building development. There was a scramble for property within a short radius of Westminster. Equally, and more important, there was a need to rebuild the City. The aristocracy, past their peak as builders and town planners, were not engaged in construction and the City became a commercial stronghold pure and simple. The Act for the Rebuilding of the City of London, approved by Parliament in 1667, was an extremely comprehensive measure, exerting the greatest ever control over building activity (see Chapter 2). As well as dealing with the rearrangement of some roads, the Act controlled the rebuilding of the houses, imposing the strictest regulations to ensure maximum fireproofing. Precise thicknesses of walls, which had to be of brick or stone, were also fixed, as were the sizes of timbers to be used for floors and roofs. Wood was banned from the outside of all houses except for beams over openings in the walls, which had to be of fire-resistant oak or, later, fir. The embellishment of exteriors was left essentially to individual taste, although the larger types of houses were required to have a balcony at first-floor level. The Act was enormously successful in promoting sound construction, partly because of its detailed provisions – it even fixed the position of cellar flaps and directed the laying of the first sewers – and partly because it merely crystallised good practice and accentuated certain desirable trends. Its effect on the design of the individual house was so profound that similar patterns appeared in other parts of the country and, in due course, in the colonies.

The Window Tax first appeared in 1695 and was increased several times in the eighteenth century, not to be repealed finally until 1857. Every inhabited house was taxed 2 shillings annually in any case, but houses worth more than £5 per annum and having more than six windows were taxed for each additional window. Hence some house-owners blocked in windows (a commoner feature in some areas, such as Bristol, than in others). Blank or dummy windows were not always a response to the tax, from which most smaller houses were exempt, but an expression of the desire for symmetry, which was an essential feature of Georgian design.

In 1707 an Act of Parliament changed the regulations affecting the external design of houses. It specified the thickness of the party wall in terraces or semidetached or back-to-back houses, and the abolition of wooden eaves cornices. From then on the typical house had a brick elevation rising to a parapet wall, the only ornamentation being the cornice, the first-floor balcony and the entrance door surround. In yet another effort to prevent the spread of fire from one house to another through window openings, a further Act of 1709 decreed that window frames be set back. At about the same time, the tall, narrow casements of the Stuart period were being replaced by the

sliding sash, which became such a *sine qua non* of Georgian fashion that even residents of labourers' cottages insisted on them, discarding casements as indications of inferior status.

Georgian house style was influenced as much by advances in technology as by changes in the law. The Industrial Revolution in the eighteenth and early nineteenth centuries brought new materials and techniques – in sources of fuel, types of brick, plasterwork, iron and glass technology, paint, plumbing and drainage systems and lighting methods, among others. These practical developments tied in with and facilitated the realisation of the ideals, or sometimes mere whims, of those who introduced, determined and promulgated new styles and tastes.

Chapter 1
The Architects and Their Styles

*'Each burst of house-building had a character of its own –
a different social character, representing a different stratum
of the national wealth and bringing into prominence
a different kind of taste.'*

William John Summerson, Georgian London
(London, Barrie & Jenkins, 1945, revised edition 1988)

The Georgian period is normally taken to refer to the reigns of George I (1714–27), his son George II (1727–60), his grandson George III (1760–1820) and George IV (1820–30). The period 1811–20, when George IV, then Prince of Wales, ruled as Regent on behalf of his insane and blind father, before himself acceding to the throne, is known as the Regency. The rule of William IV (1830–37) is often included in the term 'Georgian'. The succeeding Victorian period began in 1837 when Queen Victoria came to the throne. The neat categorisation is not merely a convenient contrivance of historians but is valid architecturally. Although Georgian style takes many forms, it is dominated by the aesthetic of Classicism.

When the Georgian period opened, the Baroque style – as expounded first and foremost by Christopher Wren (1632–1723) and his associates in the Office of Works, Nicholas Hawksmoor (1661–1736) and Sir John Vanbrugh (1664–1726) – was in gentle decline, following a brief but intense period of Baroque house building at the turn of the century. Baroque has been defined as 'a form of classicism in which emotion and sensation are allowed to control the rules of composition' (C. Aslet and A. Powers, *The National Trust Book of the English House*, Viking/National Trust, 1985). Aspects of this style were the concealed roof, achieved by either flattening it or raising a

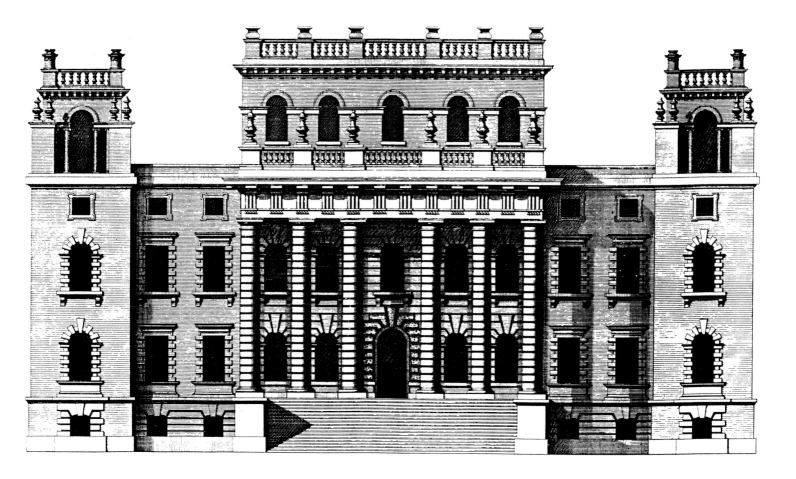

parapet; giant arched façade centrepieces; and pilasters at the extremities of the façade. By the 1730s Baroque had fallen from fashion in London, even as it continued to be a source of imaginative improvisation among small country builders. The newly ascendant Whig politics engendered a distaste for France in particular and Roman Catholicism in general, although this stance did not extend to the architecture of Ancient Rome, as interpreted by Palladio and Jones.

Palladianism was introduced into England around 1715 and championed most keenly by the 3rd Earl of Burlington and 4th Earl of Cork, Richard Boyle (1694–1753). The style was in essence an adherence to the precepts and practice of Andrea Palladio, characterised by decorum and correctness and above all a sense of proportion, as exemplified by the Palazzo Porto and the Villa Capra (or Rotonda) at Vicenza, Italy. Burlington encouraged the publication in 1715 of a new, accurate English translation of Palladio's I *Quattro libri dell'architettura* (1570) which, along with books of engravings, was crucially important in diffusing Palladian style among British architects. Palladio's rules, as presented in the first volume of the *Quattro libri*, emphasised the importance of the proportions of each part of a

building and the need to achieve harmony between these parts. Palladio affirmed the three goals of architecture as stated by Vitruvius – utility, durability and beauty – and listed various ways of attaining harmony between the various parts of a building and the whole. His second volume suggested that the kitchen, cellar and servants' quarters be located in the basement, and that the main rooms such as the library and the entrance hall, be on the main floor. The hall should be in the central axis of the building and the rooms should be arranged symmetrically.

Burlington built his own villa at Chiswick House, London (1725–9), and the Assembly Rooms in York (1731–6). More importantly, Burlington understood the need both to appeal to architects on the theoretical and didactic level, and to ensure the adoption of the new style by exerting control of the key architectural jobs in the Royal Office of Works. Burlington's protégé William Kent (1685–1748), with whom he worked closely on many projects, produced some valuable pattern books showing Inigo Jones's designs for chimneypieces, alcoves and other interior details. Isaac Ware (1706–1766) was another proponent of style by means of architectural books.

James Gibbs (1682–1754), who had travelled to Rome to

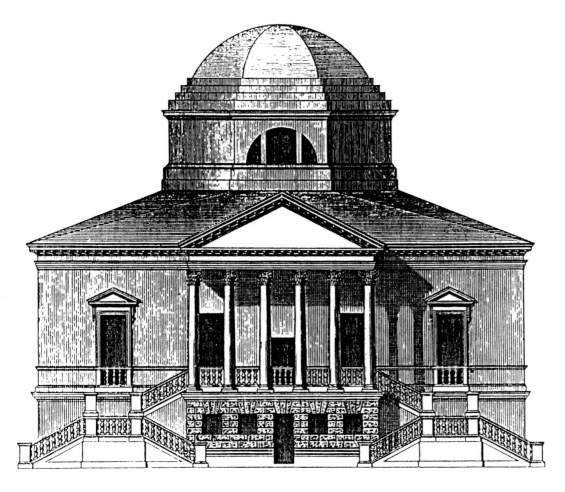

OPPOSITE PAGE: *Elevation of Eastbury in Dorset, the work of the architect Sir John Vanbrugh, as drawn by Colen Campbell in his* Vitruvius Britannicus *(1715–25).*

ABOVE: *Interiors by Inigo Jones: left, a salon; right, a great dining room; drawings taken from Colen Campbell's* Vitruvius Britannicus.

LEFT: *Lord Burlington's villa at Chiswick, designed by Inigo Jones. Notable features include the so-called Diocletian or 'Thermal' window in the octagon and the prostyle hexastyle portico at the level of the* piano nobile *(principal floor).*

train for the Roman Catholic priesthood but returned as an architect, became one of the promulgators of forms through his architectural books such as *Book of Architecture* (1728) and *Rules for Drawing the Several Parts of Architecture* (1732), in which he simplified the rules of Palladian architecture so that they could be readily understood and used by builders. He also devised the door surround with chunky quoins that became known as the 'Gibbs surround'. His influence in America was of immeasurable importance.

A close associate of William Kent was John Vardy (?1718–65), who was appointed clerk of the works at the Queen's House, Greenwich, in 1736 and also clerk at a

ABOVE: Whilst providing welcome shelter from the elements, porticos offered architects the opportunity to embellish appropriately an otherwise perhaps rather dull entrance, uplifting it to much grander proportions. These Corinthian columns enhance a residence in Virginia, USA.

RIGHT: The great sweep of the Royal Crescent, Bath, built by John Wood the Younger, 1767–75. A giant order of engaged Ionic columns rises from the piano nobile level to the crowning entablature.

succession of royal buildings, including the London palaces of Whitehall, Westminster and St James's. He was responsible for executing and perhaps modifying Kent's Horse Guards scheme. Vardy could be impeccably Palladian, but he also chose some Rococo motifs, both in his buildings and in his furniture. He began work on Spencer House, London (1755–60), but was supplanted by James 'Athenian' Stuart (1713–88), a neo-Classicist more attuned to fashionable taste. Stuart achieved an international reputation as the author, with Nicholas Revett (1720–1804), of the four-volume *Antiquities of Athens*, the first

The Palladian revival – to return to its beginnings in the early eighteenth century – had received its greatest impetus from the publication by Colen Campbell (1676–1729) of his *Vitruvius Britannicus* (*Vol. I*: 1715, V*ol. II*: 1717, *Vol. III*: 1725). Vitruvius (fl. 1st century BC) was a Roman architect and engineer, and the author of the celebrated treatise *De architectura*, a ten-volume exposition of all aspects of architecture, based primarily on Greek models and underlain by a desire to preserve the Classical tradition in the design of temples and public buildings. *Vitruvius Britannicus* appealed to British architects to free themselves of the 'odd and chimerical Beauties' of the Baroque and create a new type of building inspired by the works of the Italian Renaissance, which themselves were fine representations of classical architecture. As models, Campbell cited 100 buildings, most designed by or attributed to Inigo Jones, and this survey had an immediate effect on English architecture. Campbell provided easily copied models for a variety of Palladian building types, including the free-standing portico and the cubic hall, which would imbue buildings with the air of Classical dignity sought by the élite, and thus laid the ground for the formation of the 'national taste' for which some writers had been yearning. *Vol. I* contained designs for Wanstead House, Essex (c.1714–20; destroyed 1824), perhaps the prototype English great house, or 'house of parade'. The great house, the villa and the town house were all represented in engravings in *Vitruvius Britannicus III* of Campbell's own designs for such buildings as (respectively) Houghton Hall, Norfolk, Mereworth Castle, Kent, and Burlington House, Piccadilly. The decade of Campbell's greatest influence, 1715–25, coincided with the final stabilisation of an oligarchical society which had architectural needs that were to change little for many years and for which he provided a series of enduring solutions. Georgian Palladianism in its provincial form was rather distant from the models of Palladio or Jones but generally contained certain eclectic features such as Palladian windows or a grand Classical portico.

George Dance (1695–1768) drew on Campbell's designs for Wanstead House to produce the Lord Mayor's Mansion House, London (1735), particularly in the great hexastyle portico approached by a double flight of steps in two stages (now only one). He was succeeded as clerk of works to the City of London on his death by his younger son, George Dance (1741–1825), who was noted for his designs for the rebuilding of Newgate Gaol (1775; destroyed 1902): in his hands this became a monumental building reminiscent of Palladio's Palazzo Thiene in Vicenza, with walls of rusticated masonry (rough-hewn blocks, the joints between them being heavily emphasised with extra-deep grooves to give a feeling of strength and solidity) in rising courses of decreasing size. His skill as an urban planner came into play in 1767 with a scheme for a crescent, a circus and a square to the west of the Minories, London, along the lines laid down in Bath by the Wood family. John Wood I (1705–54)

accurate record of classical Greek architecture. His own buildings were characterised by a massiveness enlivened with simulated low reliefs and Greek motifs, and inside, with wall-painted and three-dimensional depictions of tripod perfume-burners, which became a hallmark of late eighteenth-century and Empire-style furniture and interiors. Stuart was the first architect since Ancient times to use the fluted, baseless Greek Doric order, which set a pattern for the Grecian porticoes that were to be built throughout Europe and North America in the first half of the nineteenth century.

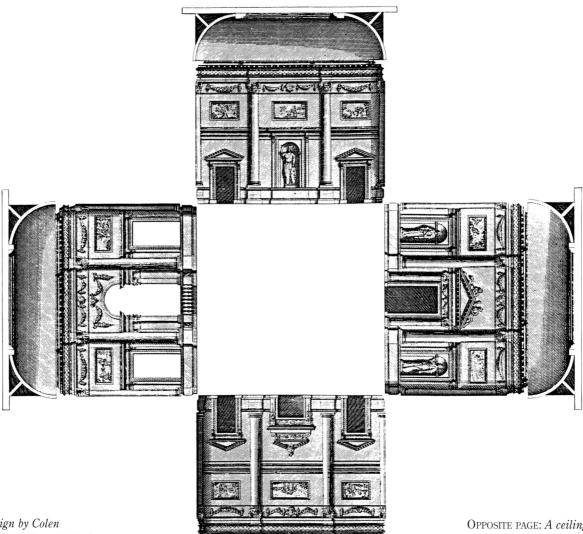

ABOVE: *Design by Colen Campbell of 'the Great Hall of my Invention being a Cube of 40 feet'. Compare the marble hall at Clandon Park, Surrey.*

OPPOSITE PAGE: *A ceiling design by Robert Adam, 1777. Ribbons, festoons and medallions were favourite Adam motifs.*

conceived of some grand adornments for what was then the inelegant country town of Bath, but for which he had high hopes as a prospective spa. Neither his Grand Circus 'for the exhibition of sports' nor his Royal Forum scheme came to fruition, but he attained the right to glorious posterity with his great enterprise, Queen Square and its vicinity (1728–36), financed by himself, where he gave a series of town houses, in his own words, 'the appearance of a palace'. His inspiration had presumably been Inigo Jones's Piazza (1631–7) at Covent Garden as well as his own reconstruction of the Roman camp at Bath. Wood's Prior Park, outside Bath, was a winged Anglo-Palladian mansion of golden Bath limestone, designed as a larger and 'juster' version of Colen Campbell's Wanstead House, beautifully united with its

magnificent hillside setting. Wood's last great design, the King's Circus (1754–c.1766), was based on his theory that God had revealed the laws of the one true architecture, first to the Druids and later to the Jews, and that perfect architectural principles could be executed in practice. His son John Wood II (1728–81) became even more famous than his father for the Royal Crescent (1767–c.1775), Bath's greatest terrace, representing the fusion of Classical palace and theatre themes with the supposed Druidical crescent. The Royal Crescent became the precedent for much ambitious urban design for nearly a century afterwards. Wood the Younger also exerted a practical and humanitarian influence with his work *Plans for Cottages*, a distinguished publication in the Palladian tradition.

Sir William Chambers (1723–96), born in Sweden of Scottish descent, having studied and travelled in Paris and Rome, arrived in London in 1755, bringing with him a liking for Continental style, which came up against a conservative British taste still steeped in the Palladian tradition. Chambers sought to reach back to select the best from recent architectural practice in Britain. The result was a sequence of villa and garden building designs, in which he revised and refined the Palladian tradition that had been established by Campbell and continued by Isaac Ware. His greatest architectural task was the building of the government offices at Somerset House, London (begun 1776); the Strand block interiors were Louis XVI in style, anticipating the work of Henry Holland at Carlton House (after 1783; destroyed 1827–8), which Holland remodelled as a new London residence for the Prince of Wales. Chambers's reputation was assured also by his *Treatise on Civil Architecture* (1759), heralded by Horace Walpole as 'the most sensible book and the most exempt from prejudices that ever was written on that science'. It was probably the finest treatise since Palladio's own, and continued to be used well into the late Victorian era. Chambers and his great rival, Robert Adam, were joint architects of the king's works. Henry Holland (1745–60) not only established his own architectural practice and entered into a partnership in 1770 with the landscape gardener and architect 'Capability' Brown, but he was also involved in speculative leasing. In the early 1770s he took a long lease on land in Chelsea and in the next 20 years laid out Hans Town, Sloane Street and Sloane Square (many of the houses on these estates were, however, replaced in about the 1890s). Irish Palladianism was virtually founded by Sir Edward Lovett Pearce (c.1699–1733), who built the Irish Parliament House. He handed the torch on to Richard Castle (?1690–1751), an Irish architect of German birth.

The Palladian style reigned supreme in Britain until about 1760, when it began to lose out to the Adam or neo-Classical style (c.1760–90). Of course each style of construction co-existed to some extent with its successors, partly because waves of fashion spread out from a centre such as London and took time to lap at the shores of distant workshops, where innovations might or might not supplant the traditional ways of thinking and doing. There was, for example, a reaction (c.1750) against red brick, but away from London this trend showed itself

more slowly or in some places not at all. The Classical repertory now diverged from the Renaissance interpretation and returned to genuine Greek forms, known from archaeological research conducted in Greece and Asia Minor. The Greek revival style was largely pioneered by Robert Adam (1728–92), who had sojourned in Italy and Spalato (Split, now in Croatia) and measured some of the ancient buildings. Greek orders replaced Roman, and mouldings became more refined. The Doric Villa at Regent's Park, London, designed by John Nash in 1828, was a later example that featured a Doric portico of four columns. The Greek revival had its greatest impact outside London, where it attained a high degree of austerity, sometimes to the point of plainness. The style of the Adam brothers – Robert and his less famous brother James (1732–94) – was refined and graceful, in contrast to the florid Rococo decoration that had enjoyed a flurry of favour in the middle decades of the eighteenth century. Unlike their predecessors who were disposed to create mansions of imposing grandeur, the Adam brothers and their followers were concerned principally with interior design, although their treatment of a series of terraced houses as a total architectural conception so as to avoid monotony while enhancing the façades, was a great contribution to that genre of building. In the houses they designed the Adams created a complete setting appropriate for the fashionable people who lived in or visited

THIS PAGE: *Some aspects of Kenwood House, north London, designed by Robert Adam: columns of the Ionic order, delicate wrought-iron verandah supports and a Classically proportioned façade.*

OPPOSITE PAGE, TOP: *Grovelands Priory, Southgate, north London was built in 1797–8 by John Nash. The house, with its Ionic columns, has been described as Nash's 'most scholarly tribute to neo-Classicism'. The house was sited amid gardens landscaped by Humphrey Repton.*

them. They paid attention not only to decoration *per se* but also to furnishings, variety in room shapes and the balance between the configuration of floors with that of walls and ceilings. They were particularly fond of curves, such that a completely rectangular room would be an exception, not the rule. One or even both ends would be elliptical or semicircular and there might be curved niches and arches, and possibly curved interior walls, as in staircase halls, for arches on landings and in passages and for low windows. Adam features such as doorways, fanlights, fireplaces, friezes and ceilings were incorporated in lesser houses by about 1780, partly as a result of the easy reproducibility of Robert Adam's invention 'compo', a plaster composition by means of which ornament could be prepared in moulds and then applied. The Adams were partial to the Venetian or Palladian window, consisting of three lights with the central light a semicircular arch; also to the doorway with engaged columns, sometimes fluted, on which a frieze rests directly; and to the Venetian doorway, in which pilasters separate the door from side lights and large fanlight arches over the whole. Adam chimneypieces and doorcases were distinctive compositions of elegance and simplicity, ornamented with plaques and such favourite motifs as guilloches, scrolls, fans, wheat-ear drops, palmettes and anthemion (Greek honeysuckle); these were derived directly from Greek, Roman and Etruscan models.

Of their own architectural philosophy, Robert and James

ABOVE: *Nash's attention to detail is evident in the simple but beautiful semicircular fanlight which nestles inside a recessed arch.*

RIGHT: *A Chinese-style design for a summerhouse by William Chambers, designer of the famous Pagoda at Kew Gardens, London.*

OPPOSITE PAGE: *Designs by Thomas Chippendale: the top two are for 'Chinese railings', the bottom two for 'Gothick frets'. The similarity is striking; both types of design were in favour during the Regency.*

Adam wrote in *The Works in Architecture*: '... we flatter ourselves we have been able to seize with some degree of success the beautiful spirit of antiquity, and to transfuse it with novelty and variety through all our numerous works.'

The last great division of Georgian architecture is usually referred to as the Regency, although it covers a period (c.1790–1830) longer than the historical Regency and a multiplicity of styles and sub-styles. On the whole, architecture at this time reflected a change in mood towards a more casual and playful, less orthodox and formal style. The Gothic style – often termed 'Gothick' to mark its brief florescence at this time and to distinguish it from its rather sterner ancestor – embodied a renewed interest in Greek architecture, and the assimilation of features from other cultures and civilisations, including Egyptian, Assyrian, Indian and later Chinese, all of which vied for the favours of housebuilders, and indeed sometimes ended up jumbled together in a single building. Straight lines gave way to curves, and Classical columns to iron balconies, although the size and layout of the houses did not change a great deal.

Regency architecture, which was primarily domestic, was not, as has been said, a definite style – rather a matter of 'trimmings', perhaps even more a cast of mind, although its manifestations are quite easy to spot. Such characteristics include: battlemented and indented parapets; pointed casement windows with tracery in the heads, margin lights and drip moulds above them; pointed doorcases with shafts or reeding up the sides and meeting at the top in an arch; hooded or unhooded wrought- or cast-iron balconies on windows and porches;

shallow, curved bays often running the full height of the building; and shallow-pitched roofs. Where the ironwork of the earlier Georgian period used Classical motifs copied from the numerous eighteenth-century pattern books, Regency ironwork used scrolls, circles and motifs derived from nature, such as flowers, leaves and vines, and later, designs based on Gothic arches, Egyptian motifs and Chinese fret patterns – all, of course, freely adapted from the originals. The 'Chinese' style, adopted also for furniture and whole buildings and now called Chinoiserie, featured, for example, balconies covered by roofs of copper or lead, in emulation of the curved roof-line of a Chinese pagoda.

Towards the end of the eighteenth century, at the same time as towns were acquiring their fanciful Regency houses, rural housing conditions had declined miserably, such that labourers were accommodated in cottages that were little more than mud hovels. The first rows of cottages, as opposed to individual ones, were built in response to the need for better housing, followed by new villages, often on the landowners' own estates. Some were laid down in a formal layout based on squares and crescents, as had been done in the towns, but this practice came to be spurned in favour of the 'picturesque' manner, in which it was thought estates and houses should look as natural as possible, with a built-in irregularity and dissimilarity designed to look accidental. James Malton suggested in his book *An Essay on British Cottage Architecture* (1798) that such buildings '... should try to preserve the vernacular by adopting the peculiar mode of building which was originally the effect of chance'. By this time, builders were not averse to re-creating in their artificial villages Swiss chalets, Italian villas, Jacobean gables, Norman window surrounds and rambling, romantic, mock-Tudor houses with pepperpot turrets and big bay windows.

One version of this trend was the cottage *orné*, a designation for romantic, often thatched houses of impractical design that paid homage to the rural idyll but were never intended for labourers, rather for the professional or merchant classes hankering after luxury in the newly fashionable country setting. Even royalty succumbed to the attraction of the pseudo-rustic cottage. Nash built Adelaide Cottage, also known as the Thatched Palace, for the Prince Regent in Windsor Park. Cottages *ornés* were not all built in the depths of the countryside but were sometimes to be found in colonies at the seaside. Often such houses – in keeping with the playful, self-demoting spirit of their owners – were full of gimmicks and novelties such as caged singing birds, palm trees and sliding mirrors. Samuel Coleridge, who lived in a real cottage, wrote disparagingly of the Devil's joy in the 'pride that apes humility'!

The Gothick style was a synthesis of Gothic, Chinese and decorative Rococo styles, popularised by pattern books such as

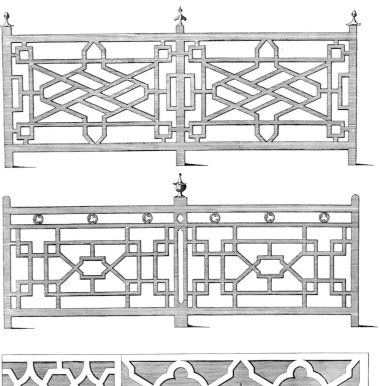

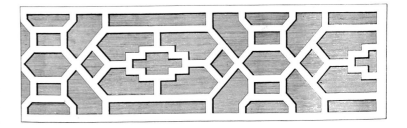

those published by Batty Langley, who attempted valiantly and with some seriousness to make sense of Gothic architecture and to promulgate its rules. Key elements of Gothick were parapets with small battlements and pointed windows. The style received a great deal of attention through the proselytising work of Horace Walpole (1717–97), 4th Earl Orford and son of Sir Robert Walpole, who spent twenty years remodelling a house at Strawberry Hill in Twickenham into an essentially Georgian house with ornament from the fourteenth and fifteenth centuries, borrowed and adapted subtly or brazenly, and reverently copied or blatantly adapted as the case demanded. A variant was the 'informal' castle, especially of the fake 'ruined' variety; but these were generally flimsily built follies that would have been

OPPOSITE PAGE: *The Royal Pavilion at Brighton, commissioned by the Prince Regent from John Nash. Finished in 1821, the building was predominantly 'Hindoo' (Indian-style) on the outside but Chinese on the inside, where the cast-iron staircases have balustrades in the form of bamboo lattice.*

BELOW: *An example of Georgian Gothick. Turrets and pointed arches were hallmarks of the style.*

amusing had they lasted long enough to be viewed by succeeding generations. Some were solid and rugged, especially when the style crossed the border into Scotland, where a version of it became known as Scots Baronial, which became the model for medium-sized houses until the end of the nineteenth century. The master of Scots Baronial, characterised by crow-stepped gables, pepperpot turrets and mullioned windows, was William Burn. Many buildings of the Regency period were, however, poorly built, and one of the greatest architects of his generation, John Nash (1752–1835), who remodelled the Royal Pavilion in Brighton and later worked on Regent's Park, London – creating terraced houses with sweeping, stuccoed colonnades – and Buckingham Palace, was posthumously accused (by James Fergusson, in *History of the Modern Styles of Architecture*, 1862) of having built anything at any price and of using cheap materials to achieve splendid effects. His preference for external stucco plasterwork was reflected in the contemporary lines:

> But is not our Nash too, a very great master,
> He finds us all brick and leaves us all plaster.

The first true villas appeared early in the eighteenth century, followed in the nineteenth by smaller copies of original Italian Renaissance buildings, usually – unlike the earlier Georgian houses – with two main storeys and lacking a basement. By the 1870s the name 'villa' – first applied to small but luxurious houses in open country, then to such houses even if surrounded by crowded urban streets – designated almost all small, semi-detached houses. A key exponent was the architect Robert Taylor (1714–88), who built a series of villas near London in the 1750s and 1760s which turned away from pure Palladianism towards more imaginative forms. Taylor invented the canted bay, which gave more space and variety to the rooms inside and an outlook on three sides. All his villas were raised on a rusticated basement which housed the domestic services, and the first and principal floor, reached by outside steps, contained four reception rooms. Isaac Ware built less innovative, if delightfully ornamented villas, for example in Bristol. By the 1770s the canted bay had ceded to the curved bay, as interpreted particularly by Samuel Wyatt (1737–1807) and his younger brother James. John Soane (1753–1837) built some modest villas, especially in East Anglia, notable for their external austerity resulting from a reductive treatment of Classicism. John Nash successfully promoted the villa as part of the Picturesque movement, creating asymmetrical, Italianate, rustic buildings, conceived as enhancements of their landscape settings.

A multitude of architectural books was published in the early nineteenth century, containing not the elevations of the old-style pattern books, but perspective views in aquatint suitable for appreciation and comprehension by the middle-class layperson. The buildings so promoted were mostly referred to as villas, but

were in fact small houses and cottages in suburban situations.

Many of these English styles had their counterparts in America, although the chronology and terminology differ. Georgian style in the colonies is often referred to as 'Colonial'; it prevailed there until the Declaration of Independence in 1776. Thereafter the term 'Federal' is applied to the architecture that corresponded with that of the later Georgian period in Britain, and included the Adam style exported to the United States during the 1780s and 1790s and the Regency style of the early nineteenth century. A fairly severe Greek revival style, popular in America in the 1820s and 1830s, may be called 'Jeffersonian' in deference to Thomas Jefferson, president of the new country, polymath and designer of his own house at Monticello, Virginia. After the war with England of 1812–14, decorative features imported from continental Europe were disseminated: the so-called 'Empire' style in fact represented a period longer than the duration of Napoleon's French empire (1804–15).

An article published in the United States in 1877 by R. S. Peabody, entitled 'Georgian Houses of New England', seems to have contained the first use in North America of the term 'Georgian' to describe what was there understood as a building type that was Classical in spirit and derived from the British architectural tradition. The author praised the 'Georgian' style as a vernacular and functional architecture that 'treated freely with

BELOW: *Empire-style design for a ceiling by Percier and Fontaine – architects, designers and decorators to Napoleon. This style, which originated in France around the time of the first French empire, in fact*

represented a period longer than the duration of Napoleon's empire (1804–15). After the war with England of 1812–14, decorative features from continental Europe found their way to America.

Palladianism had its most direct and constant influence on colonial architecture from 1750 to 1830, although some of its major principles remained in favour in the neo-Classical period, and indeed, some of its decorative elements until the end of the nineteenth century. Thus, while the style flourished in England from about 1715 to 1750, it became the dominant influence in the colonies only later. There, as elsewhere, Palladian architects were selective in their choice of Palladio's works and interpreted his techniques in the light of their own architectural background and needs.

The Greek revival in the USA began in earnest with the building (1799–1801) of the Bank of Pennsylvania in Philadelphia, capital of the nation from 1790 to 1801. Benjamin Latrobe's austere Greek Ionic temple-style building was an effectively durable symbol of the new political order. The freshness and gravity of the 'American experiment' were further expressed in the powerful Greek architecture of the Capitol in Washington DC, acclaimed by Thomas Jefferson himself as 'embellishing with Athenian taste the course of a nation looking far beyond the range of Athenian destinie'. Latrobe's pupils Robert Mills and William Strickland, and Strickland's pupil Gideon Shyrock, trod the same path, creating government buildings and monuments that echoed the Parthenon and other edifices of fifth-century BC Athens. Greek revival was also widely popular for domestic architecture in America. In 1831, the architect Thomas U. Walter remodelled a house near Philadelphia, named Andalusia, along these lines (including a wing designed in the form of the Hephaisteion) for his patron Nicholas Biddle, who was reputed to believe that 'there are but two truths in the world – the Bible and Greek architecture'!

Pattern books formed the bulk of the earliest architectural books available in North America. *The British Architect* or *The Builder's Treasury* by Abraham Swan (fl. c.1730–68), first published in London in 1745, was reissued in Philadelphia in 1775. George Washington evidently drew on this in creating the West Parlor and Banquet Room of his house at Mount Vernon, although in the latter the ornate plasterwork features representations of hoes, rakes and harrows, instead of the traditional musical instruments, presumably to accord better with the agricultural setting of the house. Exact copies of designs from the *Palladio Londinensis* – or, the *London Art of Building* – (London, 1734) by William Salmon, and from Batty Langley's *The City and Country Builder's and Workman's Treasury of Designs* (London, 1740), have been identified on houses in the eastern United States, and Langley's work clearly inspired Washington in the creation of the fine Venetian window and an elliptical window in the façade of his house at Mount Vernon. An inventory made at New Haven, Connecticut, of thirty architectural books belonging to Peter Harrison reveals how well informed was the colonial master builder of the period. Of the

regard only to comfort, cosiness, or stateliness, and with no superstitious preference for Palladio or Scamozzi [1552–1615; another late-Renaissance Italian architect whose influence permeated English architecture, largely through Inigo Jones as intermediary]'. 'Georgian' architecture in the colonial context therefore refers to the great classical tradition, rather than to a period in history.

LEFT: *View of the corridor of Independence Hall, Philadelphia, Pennsylvania, built by Andrew Hamilton who was probably inspired by the writings of James Gibbs.*

early American makers of pattern books, Asher Benjamin was probably the most influential. His popular, fully illustrated books, including *The American Builder's Companion* (Boston, 1806) and *The Practical House Carpenter* (Boston, 1830), both reflected and propagated the architectural tastes of the period. An elaborate frieze beneath the cornice of the saloon in Hyde Hall, on the shores of Otsego Lake, New York, is a copy of one of Benjamin's designs. The writings of Robert Morris (six works, published in England between 1728 and 1757) formulated precise rules about the composition of buildings, although he himself acknowledged some deviation from the Greek and Roman orders. This made his work less dogmatic and more accessible than that of his predecessors such as Lord Burlington. The buildings he designed were essentially country houses destined for the middle classes. For all these reasons, Morris's books became very popular in the colonies. There, too, the writings of James Gibbs, especially the *Book of Architecture*, did more to popularise Palladianism than those of any other writer (although in his case it was spiced with an admixture of Baroque notions). Gibbs identified the purchasers and users of his books as 'Gentlemen who may be concerned with Building, especially in the remote parts of the Country, where little or no assistance for Designs may be procured', offering drawings of buildings and ornaments 'which may be executed by any Workman who understands Lines'. These modest ambitions were exceeded: his books were the chief source for Andrew Hamilton of Philadelphia, builder of Independence Hall, and for George Washington in the building of his own house at Mount Vernon. James Hoban, a professional Irish architect, drew inspiration both from Gibbs's work and from the palace of the Duke of Leinster in Dublin when he created the White House in Washington.

From the late 1720s onwards, publications were less academic tributes to great classical truths than practical handbooks addressed to and written by tradesmen such as carpenters. These books were usually pocket-sized and inexpensive, and became highly eclectic. The publications of William Halfpenny (1728–49) were typical, offering simple techniques for designing and erecting building components such as windows, columns or arches. Such books did as much in the colonies as in Britain to spread the Palladian vocabulary beyond the large urban centres. The first architectural treatise produced in the Canadian colony was the *Précis d'architecture* in 1828, the work of the Abbé Jérome Demers: it set out a concept of French architecture in which Palladio's influence was blended with that of a number of other masters.

Besides books, architectural styles were transmitted by military architects, specifically officers of the Corps of Engineers and the Artillery, who knew only the rudiments of architecture but had learnt about perspective, the preparation of plans, elevations and sections of buildings, arithmetic and the application of mathematics to engineering. Still more important, as an influence in the construction of official residences and public and religious buildings in the colonies, were English, Scottish and Loyalist immigrants, from the late eighteenth century onwards, who brought with them knowledge of construction techniques such as ways to work in wood and stone, and of architectural models that were new to their adopted places of residence.

Chapter 2
The Plan and Façade

'Proportion is the first Principle, and proper Appropriation of the parts constitute Symmetry and Harmony.'

Robert Morris, 1751

OPPOSITE PAGE *John Wood the Younger used a form derived from Druidical tradition, combined with half the elliptical plan of the Roman Coliseum, to create the majestic sweep of the Royal Crescent (1767–c.1775), Bath's greatest terrace.*

Until well into the seventeenth century the average provincial town in England was a fairly random layout of lanes and alleys running into one or both sides of one or two main streets. Outside the 'stone belt' of the Midlands and the North, many houses were timber-framed with thatched roofs and casement windows. The risk of fire and the lack of good building timber were reasons for the rapid conversion to brick from about the 1720s onwards. London led in seventeenth-century urban development, as suburbs in what was then the 'West', such as Covent Garden and St James's Square, were laid out almost linking the City with Westminster. The houses were blocks of three or more storeys above a basement. Doorcases were of wood, but otherwise brick was used throughout, later to give way increasingly to Portland stone for grand terrace projects.

Urban terraces were not invented in the Georgian era but they and their derivatives are the period's greatest contribution to historic building types. They were uniform and symmetrical, their façades employing Classical pilasters, pedimented doors and windows, and graceful mouldings. In the case of the 'palace-fronted' terrace, which emerged by the 1720s, the entire edifice was treated as a stylistically unified composition, with stuccoed, pilastered elevations and emphasised by a central pediment and, possibly, end projections. By the end of the eighteenth century the terrace had been developed into new shapes, such as the crescent and circus, as at Bath; and new forms that deviated from the original unbroken line, such as at the famous Paragon in Blackheath, south-east London, where pairs of semidetached houses were connected by lower blocks, set further back, or by colonnades. John Nash's terraces of the 1810s and1820s marked

ABOVE: *In America, Georgian architecture inherited many ideas from Britain but also took other directions, influenced especially by Thomas Jefferson's own house, Monticello.*

Classical porticoes, as at this plantation house near Richmond, Virginia, became a feature of the grander country mansions, and later of more modest homes, too.

a return to the supremacy of the unbroken terrace front, although stuccoed rather than exposed brickwork covered the elevations, especially the basement and ground storey. The square, a late variant of the terrace, began to appear in the mid-eighteenth century. The first planned square in Dublin, Merrion Square, was begun in 1762; London's first entirely symmetrical square was Bedford Square (1775–83). By the 1820s the square having uniform terraces on each side was the most desirable of all forms of housing development.

The Georgian period was, famously, the time when spa towns such as Bath and Tunbridge Wells, and seaside resorts such as Weymouth, Brighton and Margate, were laid out, often in brick terraces. Port towns, too, were largely constructed of brick, which was readily available from other parts of the country. Later developments included the imposing and formal Edinburgh New Town, Buxton and Cheltenham where stone was the material of choice.

With industrial and commercial development putting pressure on towns, cottages for the workers were sometimes squeezed onto rented plots along alleys and passageways, or built in terraces on larger plots between lines of ribbon development. The favourite layouts favoured by small speculators were narrow, back-to-back houses in rows or grouped around courts, or sometimes, making the worst of both worlds, the two combined. When the houses were built in terraced rows, the streets themselves tended to be narrow. In Preston, Lancashire, in working-class districts, some streets were only 9 feet (about 2.75m) wide. In the last decades of the eighteenth century and the first decades of the nineteenth, the better houses faced principal streets. Again, in the smaller, poorer developments, these houses sometimes had just one room up, for sleeping, and one room down – a 'house place' – or, if somewhat larger, two bedrooms, a living room and a corner for a scullery. The rooms were perhaps 3 by 4 yards (approx. 2.75 x 3.6m) in area. Behind this row and backing onto it was another row of houses: neither could thus have windows except to the front, and through ventilation was impossible. The back row looked onto a much narrower street, which served not only as a thoroughfare for the residents but also as a dumping-ground for the rubbish of the neighbourhood. In the centre of each row of houses there might be a group of privies, in a space about a yard (1m) wide. The sleeping rooms that were built over these privies were unventilated and could obviously become very smelly.

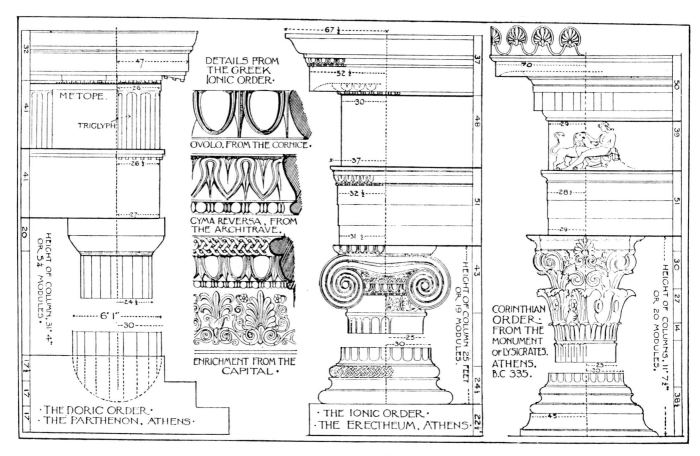

Doric Order

OPPOSITE PAGE: *From the seventeenth century onwards British, and later American, architects emulated classical styles. They were particularly drawn to the elegant austerity and precision of Greek columnar architecture, of which details of the three principal styles – Doric, Ionic and Corinthian – are illustrated here.*

LEFT: *Thomas Chippendale's famous* The Gentleman and Cabinet-Maker's Director *of 1762 was one of the first pattern books, which offered principles as well as practical designs for the builder, cabinetmaker or upholsterer.*

BELOW: *A Georgian stone terrace in Bath, with classically pedimented doors and an iron railing fronting the basement 'area'.*

RIGHT: *Typical Georgian stone terraces in Bath, with the tallest windows on the first floor and a row of dormers in the roof.*

LEFT: *Classically proportioned terraced housing in Brighton. The windows set into arched recesses add some interest to the otherwise starkly plain exterior.*

BELOW: *Regency terraces in the seaside town of Brighton. Steps lead to the front door on the raised main floor, which is overhung by a shallow awning.*

Legislation, Taxation and Economics

The Rebuilding Act of February 1667 that followed the Great Fire of London dealt with the rearrangement of some roads, imposed the strictest fire regulations hitherto, and specified four classes of new house that were to be allowed in London. Houses of the first and least sort, facing 'by-lanes', were to be two storeys high, the rooms on both floors being 9 feet (approx. 2.75m) high. Houses of the second sort, fronting 'streets and lanes of note' or the River Thames, were to be three storeys high, the rooms on the lower floors being 10 feet (approx. 3m) high, those on the upper floor 9 feet. Houses of the third sort, fronting the 'high and principal streets' (only six streets were so classified), had to be four storeys high. A fourth class was reserved for 'houses of the greatest bigness', which did not front the street but lay behind in their own grounds: these houses, too, were limited to four storeys. In houses of the third and fourth classes, the two lower floors were to be 10 feet high, the third 9 feet and the upper floor 8½ feet (approx. 2.5m). Cellars and garrets were permitted in all cases, always with a minimum height of 6½ feet (approx. 2m). Basements represented a shallow excavation only. The widths of the frontages were generally not less than 14 feet (approx. 12.3m) for the first sort of house; 18–24 feet (5.5–7.5m) for the second sort; and 30–40 feet (9–12m) or more for the third and fourth sorts. The Act was based on the principle that new houses were built as continuous terraces fronting both sides of a street. Since London's streets could not always be made to conform to the definitions of the Act, a good deal of freedom was in effect permitted.

The standardisation of construction was a very important feature of the Act. Walls were required to be of brick or stone, and their precise thicknesses at various heights were fixed, as were the sizes of timbers to be used for floors and roofs. No wood was to be placed within 12 inches (30.5cm) of the front of any chimneys, and all joists at the rear were to be at least 6 inches (15cm) from the flue. The use of timber was banned inside any chimney or in the walls around flues, as also from the outside of all houses, except for beams over openings in walls.

THIS PAGE: *The classical influences of ancient Greece are clearly evident in these designs for a window and a doorcase.*

N.º III

Ionic Order

T. Chippendale inv. et del   Pub. according to Act. of Parliam. 1738   T. Muller sculp.

LEFT: *Georgian architecture was based on the ancient system of Classical 'orders'. This engraving of the Ionic order is taken from Chippendale's* Gentleman & Cabinet-Maker's Director *of 1762.*

OPPOSITE PAGE: *Georgian terraces in London. All feature iron balconies, a raised front door, and iron railings separating the pavement from the sunken 'area'.*

RIGHT: *Iron balconies embellish the first-floor windows of this London house.*

ABOVE: *Rear view of London terraces, presenting a more confused exterior than the elegantly simple front elevations. In Georgian times roads were often artificially built up, while the rears of the building plots were at a lower level.*

RIGHT: *The Grecian orders of Classical or columnar architecture were the Doric, the Ionic and the Corinthian, each displaying precisely determined characteristics, usually based on the lower diameter of the column. The Ionic order had columns 9–9¹/₂ diameters in height, with 24 flutings. The capital consisted of a pair of double scrolls or volutes supported by echinus (convex projecting) moulding.*

BELOW: *Roman architecture was similar in plan to Greek but usually larger in scale and more ostentatious in its mouldings and ornaments. The Romans added the Tuscan and the Composite orders to the three existing orders.*

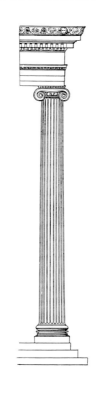

The requirements of the Act were followed by and large throughout the Georgian period, leading to an overall raising of construction standards, although in fact the Act merely confirmed what was already the subject of good practice, thus perpetuating the best of existing notions and methods. A certain uniformity and somewhat boring predictability in building style were perhaps inevitable consequences, although flexibility of interpretation usually meant that orderliness was achieved without too much monotony.

The better-class terraced houses nearly always had a 24-foot (7m) frontage and the same depth, making a square floor plan. This pattern was repeated not only in London but ultimately throughout the British Isles. The plots were generally long and narrow. The garden level at the rear was usually at about natural ground-level, while the road in front was built up to an artificial higher level, creating the need for an open 'area' in front of the house to permit light to enter basement windows. The wall around this area helped to shore up the road in front, where there was generally a railing to prevent visitors to the house from falling into the area itself. In certain parts of London's West End the legacy of this practice remains in the form of discrepancies in level between streets which adjoin each other.

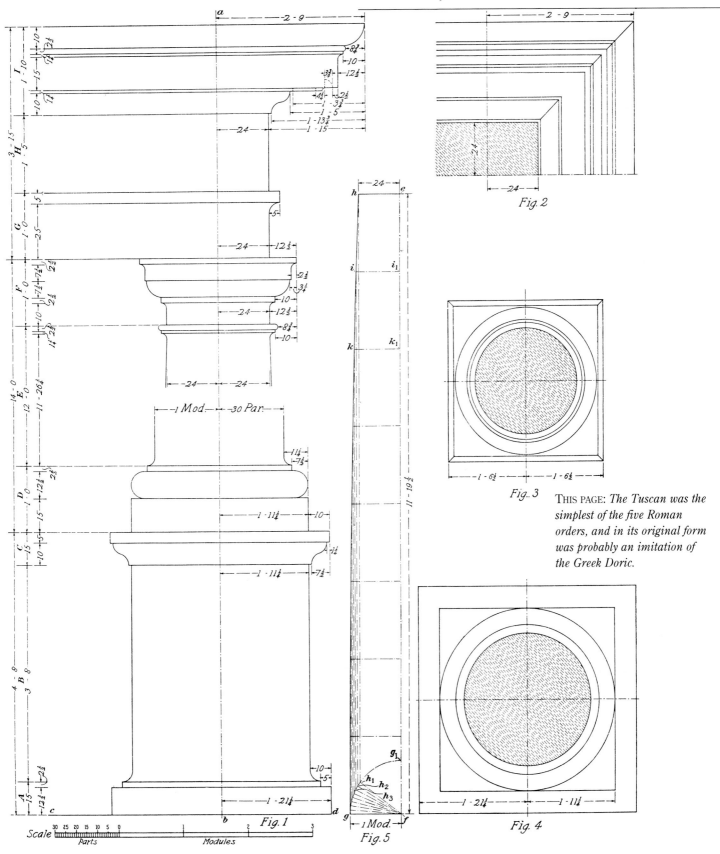

Fig. 2

Fig. 3

THIS PAGE: *The Tuscan was the simplest of the five Roman orders, and in its original form was probably an imitation of the Greek Doric.*

Fig. 1

Fig. 5

Fig. 4

Scale

Parts   Modules

BELOW: *A palace-fronted terrace at Brighton, with an iron balcony running continuously along the façade.*

RIGHT: *Mathematical tiles became popular, particularly in fashionable seaside towns (here at Brighton), by the end of the eighteenth century. They were ceramic tiles with large pegs at the rear, which were nailed in overlapping layers on a vertical wall and resembled brick courses.*

LEFT: *The Georgian period was the time when seaside resorts such as Brighton (seen here) were laid out, very often in streets of brick terraces of three or more storeys. The palace-fronted terrace was conceived as a single, harmonious unit of rigid symmetricality.*

BELOW: *Unusual enclosed balconies above the porticoed entrances gave a wide view of the seafront in these attractive Brighton terraces.*

In 1707 the fireproofing provisions of the 1667 Act were strengthened when external wooden cornices were banned; and in 1709 further legislation stipulated that sash boxes be recessed at least 4 inches (10cm) from the outer faces of the principal elevation. These Acts applied to London only, although of course their provisions were taken up outside the capital, not only in Britain but also eventually in the colonies.

The Building Act of 1774, drafted by the architects Robert Taylor and George Dance, was intended to ensure sound construction and the most stringent fire-prevention measures, and applied throughout the country. This time new houses were classified into four types, or 'rates' – the first time legislation had accorded status to housing. The fourth and lowest rate was a house worth less than £150 (its annual value in ground rent) and occupying less than 350 square feet (32sq m). Third rate houses were worth between £150 and £300, with a floor space of 350–500 square feet (32–46sq m). Second rate houses were valued between £350 and £850 and had a floor space of between 500 and 900 square feet (46–84sq m). First rate houses were valued at over £850 with a floor space of over 900 sq feet (84sq m). There were two other rates applicable to detached houses. Each class or rate had to conform to its own structural code with respect to foundations, thicknesses of external and party walls and the positions of windows in outside walls. For all rates, the Act stipulated that all external window joinery be hidden behind the outer skin of masonry, as a precaution against fire. The Act's constraints on the main fabric and structure of the house were such that scope for inspiration or initiative were also curbed. During the next half-century or so, second-, third- and fourth-rated houses became standardised throughout the country. Though the dimensions of the buildings were now assured, no legislation was available to limit occupancy. Smaller houses that yielded low rents were increasingly shoddily built, and the combination of overcrowding and poor-quality housing led to a severe decline in general living conditions.

The 1774 Act also restricted the use of exterior projecting cornices and exposed timberwork, and required window frames, apart from the sill, to be entirely concealed in brick reveals, or recesses. Bay windows and shop fronts had to project no more than 10 inches (25cm) from the face of the building (the true Georgian bay was thus much shallower than its twentieth-century 'Georgian-style' counterpart). As the Act did not, however, relate the height of the houses to the width of the street, many disproportionately large houses were built on streets that accordingly became sunless and gloomy.

This positive legislation was counterbalanced by other government measures that made life difficult for builders. To raise revenue in 1766 the government extended the Window Tax of 1696 to include all houses with seven or more windows; and in 1784 to include houses with six or more windows. A Brick Tax was imposed, also in 1784, to provide funds to fight the

BELOW: *The Building Act of 1774 classified new houses into four types, called 'rates', in order to ensure sound construction and stringent fire-prevention measures. A house rated first class (below) was valued at over £850 and had a floor space of over 900 square feet (84sq m).*

BELOW: *A house rated second class was worth between £350 and £850, in terms of its annual value in ground rent, and had a floor space of 500–900 square feet (46–84sq m).*

ABOVE AND LEFT: *Houses rated third and fourth class were the smaller types, worth, respectively, £150–£300 and less than £150; and occupying, respectively, 350–500 square feet (32–46sq m) and less than 350 square feet (32sq m). The dimensions of all rates of houses were standardised.*

BELOW AND RIGHT: *The* piano nobile *(principal floor) was that on which the main reception rooms may have been situated, and received the most attention from architects.*

BOTTOM RIGHT: *The curved bays on these Regency buildings in Brighton admitted plenty of light and gave unrestricted views to the residents.*

LEFT AND BELOW: *Tall terraces with large windows, often within curved bays, were typical of Georgian seaside housing, as here at Brighton.*

RIGHT: *Chippendale's* Director *illustrated the proportions and dimensions of the Corinthian order. The order was not much used by the Ancient Greeks, but it was characteristically refined and delicate in detail, and was thus an attractive model for Georgian architects.*

BELOW: *The Monument of Lysicrates, Athens, built 335* BC, *was a Corinthian building.*

MONUMENT OF LYSICRATES. ATHENS. B.C. 335.

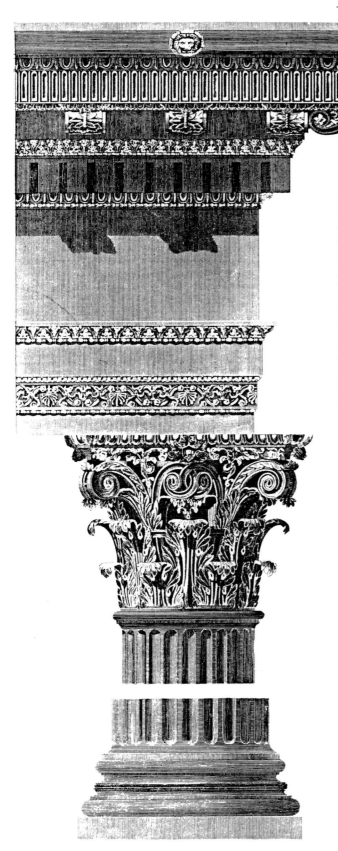

LEFT: *Features of the Corinthian order were the rich entablature; the deep and elaborate cornice; and the capital, a little greater than a diameter in height, and enriched with acanthus foliage and spiral volutes.*

Americans in their War of Independence. As the tax – which itself doubled for small bricks from 2s 6d per 1,000 in 1784 to 5s per 1,000 in 1803 – related to numbers, builders retaliated by developing bricks that were abnormally and inadvisedly large – up to twice the normal size in Leicestershire and Hertfordshire. Another consequence of the Brick Tax was that tile-hanging became popular on walls or timber framework, since roof tiles were untaxed. Furthermore, other cladding materials might be chosen in preference to brick, most frequently weatherboarding, which made use of painted or tarred softwood boards, laid horizontally and overlapping at the edges. The Napoleonic Wars, which dragged on from 1793 to 1814, were a huge drain on the nation's resources, and the price of land and materials rose to the extent that building costs almost doubled during the period. Fir and pine, which had become the most widely used timbers and were imported from Scandinavia and America, also became scarce as a result of the wars.

Builders accordingly cut corners. Party and rear walls were often erected by less skilled workers before experienced bricklayers came in to add the front wall, the only area of brickwork that would be exposed to public scrutiny. This practice sometimes left walls not bonded together satisfactorily or, in some cases, at all. To shore up brickwork, bonding timbers were sometimes placed just above the footings, a practice that failed singularly when the timbers started to decay, allowing the whole building to settle. The architect Isaac Ware wrote in 1735 that some builders 'have carried the art of building slightly so far that their houses have fallen before they were tenanted'. Equally, however, it has to be recognised that some of those houses built on the cheap in the eighteenth century are still standing.

In the late eighteenth century two significant changes to house exteriors occurred. First, tiles began to be superseded by slates, notably from the Penrhyn and Dinorwic quarries. Slates were commonly laid in diminishing courses, which transferred a good deal of the weight of the roof covering from the apex to the outer walls and permitted a shallower roof pitch and a greater surface area from which rainwater could run off. Second, walls were increasingly often covered with mathematical tiles, which were in fact false bricks made of ceramic, nailed to the battens or to the timber framework of the house and with the joints pointed to resemble brick courses.

OPPOSITE PAGE: *A monumental gateway frames and leads onto restrained terraces at Regent's Park, London.*

LEFT: *This building in Regent's Park, London, with its hexagonal tower above a pedimented doorway, borrows heavily from Classical models.*

ABOVE: *Ornamented columns support the balcony of this imposing house situated in Regent's Park, London. The main window on the first floor is topped by a semicircular fanlight.*

BELOW: An extract from Chippendale's Director illustrating the Composite order, as used principally in the architecture of Italy.

OPPOSITE PAGE: In Roman amphitheatres and consequently in Georgian buildings, orders were sometimes placed above one another, an arrangement called superposition. The upper diameter of each shaft was made equal to the lower diameter of the one above it, as if they constituted a single tapering column.

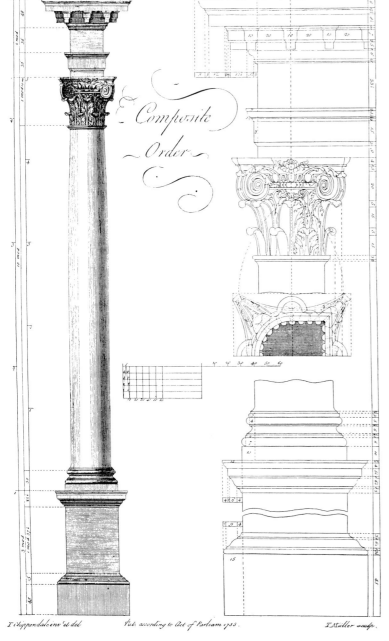

T. Chippendale inv' et del.   Pub. according to Act of Parliam 1755.   T. Muller sculp.

Plans and Elevations – Urban Housing

The disposition of rooms in a terraced house obviously varied according to the number of floors. Since terraces were devised to accommodate the greatest number of people on a limited site, each house was deep and narrow. All except the poorest houses had basements. The rear led directly into a court and then sometimes up some steps to a yard or garden. As for the plan of the most basic house, as John Summerson wrote in *Georgian London*, 'nothing could be simpler': one room at the back and one at the front on each floor, with a passage and staircase at one side at the rear, slightly cutting into the area of the rooms on that floor but allowing the front room on the upper floors to be the full width of the house. The ground floor of a somewhat larger house, entered by the front door, typically contained a dining room, a parlour and a library. The kitchen might be to the rear or in the basement, along with a cellar and servants' quarters. Bedrooms occupied the first floor; in the grander house sometimes accompanied by sitting rooms. The second floor was given over to further, minor bedrooms or to servants' quarters if these were not in the basement or in the roof. The larger house had, by law after 1667, to have an external balcony at first-floor level, a feature that continued throughout the Georgian period. Dog-leg staircases were a means of making use of a limited space. The flues serving the fireplaces had to be placed within the party walls, often back to back with adjacent houses. 'The story of the better class London house,' wrote Summerson, 'is a story of ingenious variation within the inflexible limits of party walls.' It was early discovered that an annexe could be built at the back so as to provide additional room space while not blocking the window area of the main back room. Far and away the preferred solution to pressure on space, however, was to extend upwards rather than outwards. This gave nearly all houses of this era, from humble cottages to large fashionable houses on estates, what has been termed their 'insistent verticality'. A concomitant was a new liking for differentiation between the back and the front of the house; by the early nineteenth century, the front had more modern and better quality spatial arrangement, detailing and workmanship than the back.

In the late seventeenth century the 'double-pile' house plan emerged, and this became the culmination of vernacular small-house planning about a century later. The double-pile plan was so-called because the house was two rooms deep at each floor level. Tall rooms on each of two or more storeys gave the solid cubic shape that characterises detached houses of this type and period. Living room and parlour were usually at the front, which was entered by a slightly off-centre door, and kitchen and dairy or scullery at the rear, with the staircase between them. There would be four bedrooms on the first floor and often a garret or attic in the roof space. There might be a cellar under part or all of the ground floor. The front entrance opened into one corner of the living room and there was also a back door into the kitchen.

OPPOSITE PAGE, TOP: *A 'house of parade', the grandest of Palladian house types, with an imposing columned portico framed by lower lateral wings.*

OPPOSITE PAGE, BOTTOM LEFT: *This house has a rigidly horizontal façade, with engaged columns which rise through two storeys, and also a starkly horizontal delineation between the upper storeys.*

OPPOSITE PAGE, BOTTOM RIGHT: *An interesting arrangement of windows adorns the façade of this house, including, on the top floor, a circular window called an oculus.*

LEFT: *Detached Ionic columns with their double scrolls support an elaborate pediment featuring a continuous frieze. The statues used in this order were often female figures clad in drapery which had vertical folds that echoed the flutings of the column.*

Fireplaces were usually sited in side walls, although sometimes they were back to back in the centre of the plan on the partition walls dividing front from back rooms.

The Palladian style was employed in the rural houses of the more well-to-do, and transposed, with adaptations, to the urban setting. In a characteristic Palladian house a horizontal division of the façade was emphasised by the cornice and the course delineating the basement. Other Palladian features were the arrangement and size of the windows (rectangular on the main floor, small and square on the top floor), the raised basement of rusticated stone, and the central portico. In the early nineteenth century colonial builders favoured the designs of James Gibbs, which were simple, elegant and adaptable. Typical features were a projecting frontispiece, sometimes of rusticated stone, and perhaps surmounted by a pediment, quoins, keystones over openings, an oculus (round window) in the pediment, a raised basement and a course delineating the two storeys. The 'house of parade', the grandest of Palladian house types, was distinguished by a central porticoed block framed by lower lateral wings, to which it was linked by single-storey passages or colonnades; the imposing columned portico reached by a flight of steps the height of the ground storey; engaged columns rising from the ground storey up the principal storeys of the façade; the use of the ground storey of the main block, often of rusticated stone, as a basement on which the reception floor, the *piano nobile*, was raised; frequent use of Venetian and triangular-pedimented windows; and the absence of superfluous ornament. Later and more modest detached houses retained some of these features, of which the most important was the symmetrical and dignified appearance, especially at the front facing the approach.

The family generally occupied the main floor, where, in a large house, the saloon was surrounded by a circuit of rooms for entertaining. Bedrooms and a chapel might be on the same floor or in separate wings; or the bedrooms might be on the first floor, in which case they were usually at the front of the house (see also Chapters 3 and 4). In poorer houses the layout of rooms

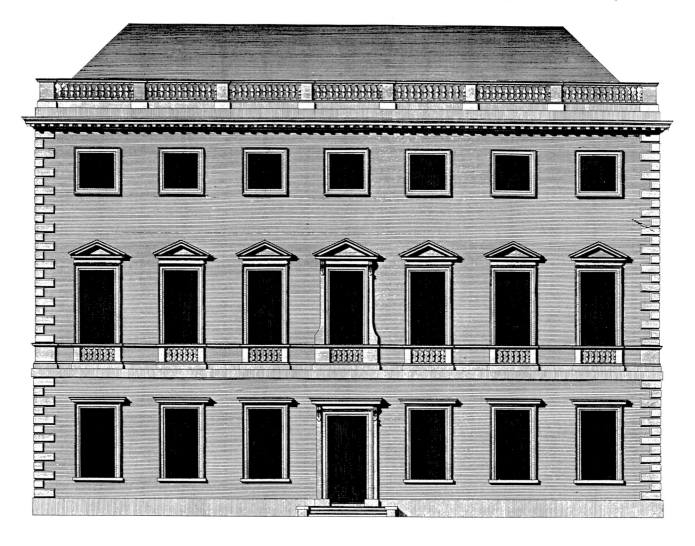

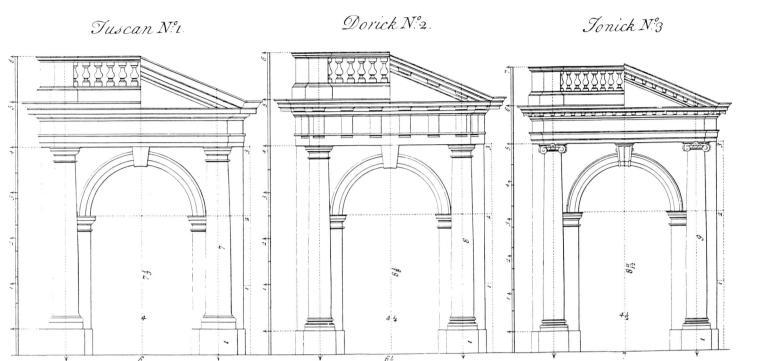

Tuscan Nº1.   *Dorick Nº2.*   *Jonick Nº3*

OPPOSITE PAGE: *Horizontal features, such as the stone courses delineating the ground and first floors, demonstrate the bare bones of Palladianism in the Duke of York's palace in Pall Mall, London. Monotony was frequently a charge laid against such buildings as the Georgian period wore on and construction became standardised.*

ABOVE: *A comparison of three of the five orders of antiquity, here showing details of parapets, pediments, entablatures, columns, keystones and arches.*

LEFT: *Foots Cray, Kent, a typical Palladian house, with a columned portico which is reached by a flight of steps the height of the ground storey, also engaged columns at the extremities of the façade, and an oculus in the domed roof.*

RIGHT: *Venetian windows flanking the front door and arched windows on the first floor embellish this façade. The pediment over the door is unusual in that it is broken at the lower edge to make way for the arched fanlight.*

BELOW: *It was common practice for rural houses to be given two storeys, having tall rooms with symmetrically arranged sash windows.*

LEFT: *Whitewebbs House, on the outskirts of north London, features a recessed entrance and colonnaded wings. The roof is strewn with chimney stacks.*

BELOW: *The green of the front door was a popular feature of rural cottages in the Georgian period. Verdigris, a fine, deep green derived from corroding copper, was one of the more expensive oil-based paints.*

might be similar, but instead of occupying the entire house a family might occupy one floor only.

Adam exteriors were rather simple compared with those of Palladian houses. The emphasis was on well proportioned windows and a hidden roof, in deference to Roman tradition. The façade was usually furnished with a cornice, perhaps with a shallow parapet or stone balustrade above it, and a central pediment. The Venetian window or any other triple window was a common feature of houses of this period. The Adam brothers were responsible for popularising the use of *stucco duro*, scored with lines and painted, on the ground floor of brick exteriors, where it simulated the rusticated stone below the main floor of Palladian mansions.

From the late seventeenth century into the nineteenth, a typical middle-class detached house of two principal storeys comprised a small entrance hall, flanked by dining room and drawing room and leading to the staircase hall; under the staircase, a door would give access to the basement and another to the rear of the house; a morning room behind the drawing room; a passage behind the dining room leading to the housemaid's pantry, with the servants' back stairs ascending from the passage; over the dining room and the drawing room would be the two main bedrooms, with a dressing room between them sited over the entrance hall; a bedroom over the morning room; across the stair landing, a passage leading to a small bedroom or linen room; the second flight of the servants' back stairs ascending from the passage to the attic floor. In some houses there were no side passages, the servants using the family's staircase to the first-floor landing, from which a secondary staircase led to the attic. In the more ambitiously designed house, the entrance lobby and staircase hall might be of the same width, the two forming a rectangular hall the depth of the house. Access to the basement and the servants' stairs would be from a passage at the far end of the staircase hall; and access to the attic from the first floor would be by a flight of stairs from a side corridor between front and back rooms and connecting with the stairs from the ground passage. In early Georgian times it was fashionable for town houses to have double doors between front and back rooms on the ground floor, if there was no intervening passage, so that they could be opened to make one large reception room.

The villa was typically a small country house, usually the

BELOW: *Rorkby Park, Yorkshire, designed by William Wakefield, has the rusticated stone basement and quoins much favoured by Georgian architects.*

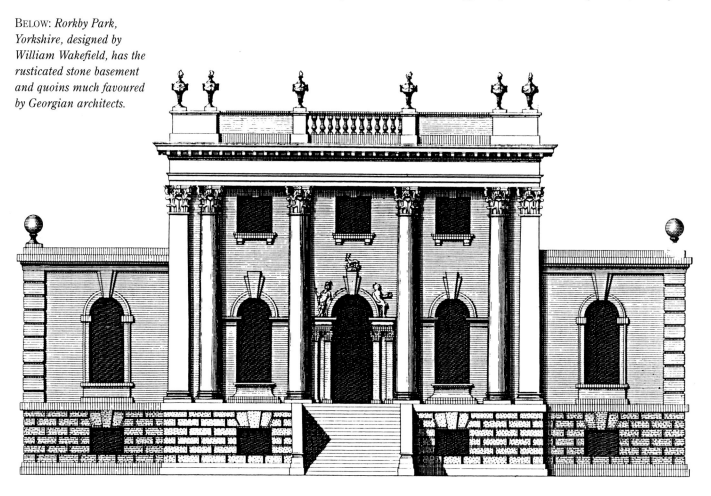

secondary seat of landed family, but often in a suburban setting. The plan, according to John Harris (*The Palladians*, 'RIBA Drawings Series', London, Trefoil Books, 1981), 'must be square, with a compact arrangement of rooms grouped round a staircase, and expressed on the two main exterior façades in a 1–3–1 rhythm of windows or bays.' In its semidetached and far more modest form, it was perhaps the characteristic expression of Regency housing. In that case it was usually narrow, with a frontage consisting of a single room and the entrance hall. Each storey was two rooms deep, and there might be a projection at the rear containing a small closet for each floor. Where overcrowding was an issue, these houses often rose to three or even four storeys, in which case the dining room was normally on the ground floor, the drawing room on the first floor and the kitchen in the basement. The rooms were high and well proportioned, with tall windows particularly to the first floor.

Regency Gothick façades displayed characteristics such as battlemented or indented parapets; pointed casement windows with margin lights (small panes bordering the main large ones of the window) and drip moulds over them; and porches surrounded by narrow shafts and pointed doorcases also with narrow shafts or reeding at the sides that met at the top of the arch. A late resurgence of interest in Greek styles, after 1815, produced façades that often had porches employing the Greek Doric or Ionic orders; a dwarfed attic storey; a low-pitched pediment and shallowly recessed windows. A shortlived Regency style was the Egyptian, rarely used for a complete exterior, but recognisable by a façade and windows in the form of one side of a truncated pyramid, and often by Egyptian ornament such as the winged solar disc. Fashionable Regency exteriors were covered all over with smooth stucco, painted cream or beige. Sometimes this was a means of disguising shoddy workmanship. It was also a way of avoiding the Brick Tax; others included the use of tiles or slates hung on a timber framework, or of timber on all except the brick ground floor. Stucco pilasters or merely pilaster-like projections were a feature of Regency houses. Many unstuccoed houses in and around London were faced with greyish-yellow brick. Other Regency features frequently seen are the curved bay, between one and four storeys high, or a semi-hexagonal bay; and graceful ironwork balconies to upper windows, sometimes extending the whole width of the house.

BELOW: *An interesting example of the interplay between horizontal and vertical features in this Palladian-style house.*

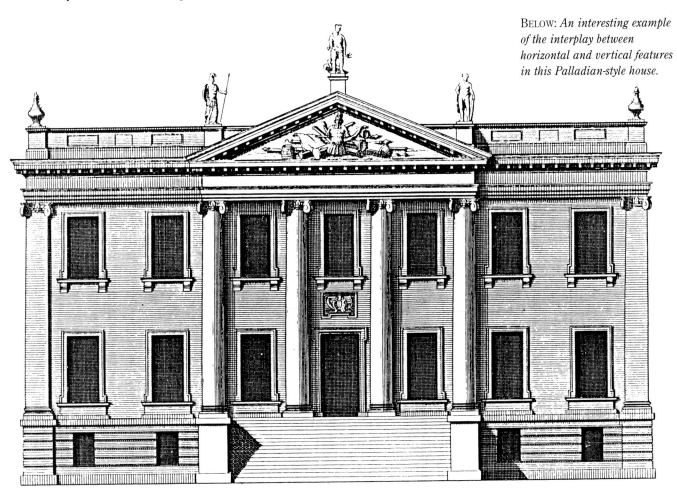

THIS PAGE: *The rural houses shown here display a number of Georgian features, including Venetian (tripartite) windows, horizontal stone courses, an arched niche and a portico with triangular pediment.*

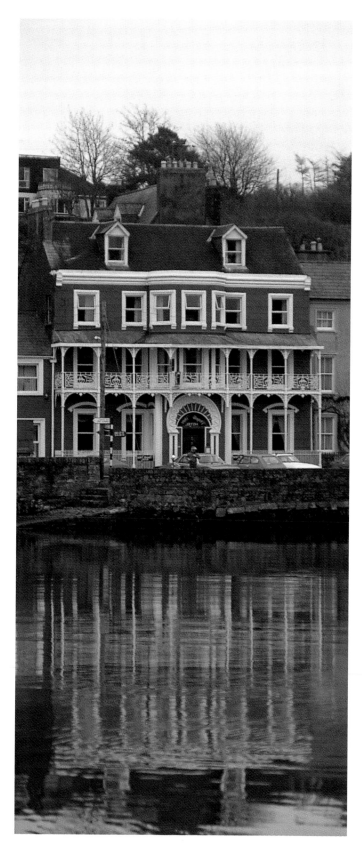

LEFT: *The roofed balcony is a delicate feature of this house situated in Kinsale, Southern Ireland. The façade, with its columns on the lower floors and two dormer windows, gives the impression of a triangle tapering towards the top.*

BELOW: *A house in Bristol with an unusual arched bay descending to the basement.*

By the end of the Georgian period, the double-fronted suburban house had become the norm. It had a block plan, a symmetrical, well proportioned front carrying a heavy cornice, a raised bay window on the reception floor over a basement that was perhaps rusticated, and steps leading up to a Classical front porch. Classical orders had disappeared from the façade and panes of sheet glass were now so large that glazing bars were thin enough to be of metal. Stucco was no longer applied to the entire façade but was normally restricted to cornice, quoins, basement, windows and porch. Indoors, the accommodation was neatly disposed on either side of the entrance lobby and staircase. This period marked the end of an era in design that was characterised by harmony between architecture and function and the utmost appropriateness to the structure of a building of its ornamental detail.

Plans and Elevations – Rural Housing

The Georgian period as a whole was a time when too many people were chasing too little work, and when, especially after about 1760, prices were rising to the extent of causing what has been termed the 'semi-pauperisation of the population of rural England'. The Industrial Revolution brought little benefit to most ordinary people before 1800; indeed, some of the apparent benefits proved retrograde for a time, as when the introduction

of the water closet led to the rapid contamination of the Thames, from which London drew its water supply. A visitor touring England in 1810–11, however, reported seeing houses in good repair and 'a great degree of ease and comfort among the lower ranks' (Louis Simond: *An American in Regency England: The Journal of a Tour in 1810–11*, ed. Christopher Hibbert, 1968). Builders had to rely, by and large, on locally available materials, until the building of canals went some way towards facilitating the transport of materials. Canal 'rage' did not reach its peak until the 1790s, however, and even when, at the culmination of the enterprise, there were 4,000 miles (6,400km) of inland waterways, the system did not open up every area of the country to communication – and besides, canal water was usually 'black as the Styx and absolutely pestiferous'. Meanwhile, coaches and horse-drawn railways were the only other means of carrying goods from door to door. Again, the widespread use of such materials as ironwork and artificial stone had to wait on the development of mass production and standardisation.

In the country cottages of rural England in pre-Georgian and early Georgian times, the great farm kitchen had been the centre of the household – the 'houseplace', in northern parlance. This was the focus of the lives of family and hired hands, though they usually ate different food at separate tables. As people became more prosperous, a separate

RIGHT: *Myddelton House, Enfield, was built in 1821 for the Bowles family. Here the windows decrease in height from the ground upwards.*

OPPOSITE PAGE: *Bullstrode House, north of London: wings project in front of the façade, which is bare of any superfluous ornament. The* piano nobile *boasts tall windows.*

sitting room, perhaps even a best parlour for entertaining, began to appear. Where earnings were low, however, housing tended to be poor, consisting of thatched structures made from any local material, or even of mud hovels. Cottages might have a day room and two bedrooms, a pantry, fuel house and small garden and (for example in Dorset) an adjoining pigsty. Some cottages were owned by their inhabitants, others rented; it was not uncommon for labourers to have to pay nearly a fifth of their earnings on rent.

From the basic two-unit, single-storey plan that was the oldest type of English house, the tendency in rural areas was for usable floor area to increase. Farmhouses more commonly had two storeys, plus garrets and cellars. From a single retiring room there developed multiple bedrooms, a parlour and a dining room, even a study, as well as pantries and granaries. Comfort improved, as did heating, which allowed more rooms to be usable. The single hearth that existed in houses subject to the Hearth Tax in the late seventeenth century had been

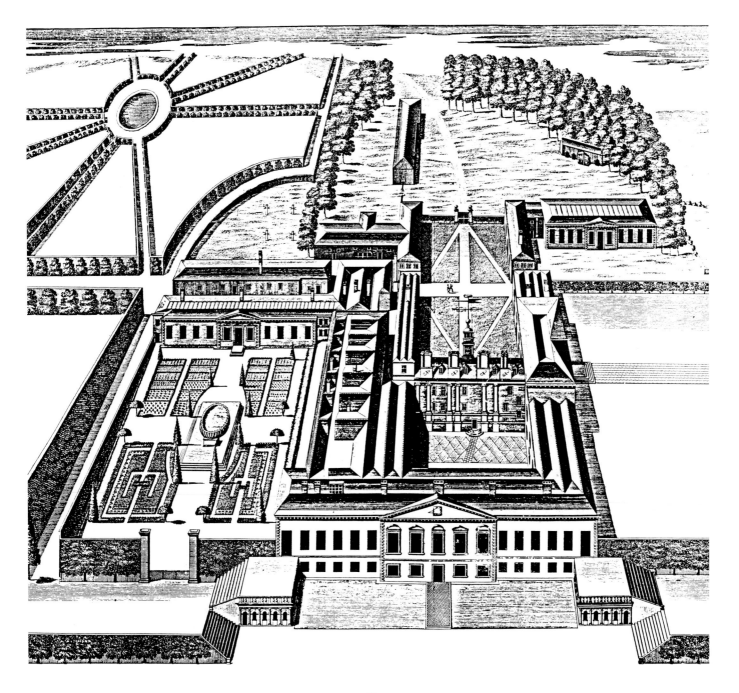

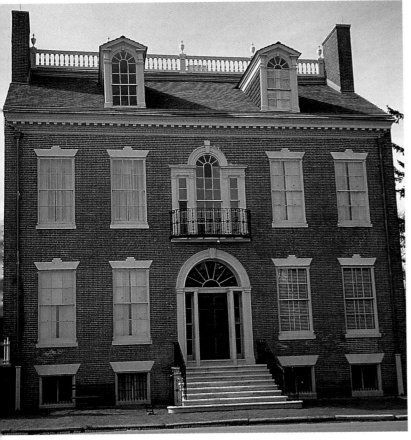

OPPOSITE PAGE: *The Colonial style was the counterpart in North America of the Georgian style, with Palladian features such as regularly proportioned façades, sash windows and pedimented doorways. Roofs tended to be of steeper pitch than in England. Large central chimneys were also common.*

THIS PAGE: *External shutters frame the windows of these houses in Williamsberg, Virginia, USA; the dark colour of those on the house below is more likely to be authentic than the stark white seen on the left. Small Classical porticoes were favoured as a means of emphasising the entrance.*

replaced, a century later, by at least four considerably more efficient fireplaces. There was movement towards privacy: family and servants were able to maintain separate zones even in quite small houses, and rooms no longer opened off each other but off corridors or landings on staircases. Household activities that had previously been performed outdoors or in rough shelters were generally brought into the house proper – thus kitchens, sculleries and dairies were accommodated indoors, if in separate wings or subsidiary sections of the house.

The Colonies

In America, Colonial and Federal style houses were very similar to Georgian houses in Britain, although there was inevitably a time lag in the take-up of innovations and fashions. Wood was used more than stone, and the houses sometimes hung with tiles or shingle. For much of the eighteenth century, in more rural areas, houses were asymmetrical, with leaded casement windows and high, gabled roofs, usually steeply pitched. Large chimneys – central in New England, at the gabled end in the south – were standard. The houses of the north-east were often

RIGHT: *The east façade of the President's House, Washington DC, as it was in 1823. Thomas Jefferson, himself a distinguished architect, made many improvements to the house during his incumbency 1801–9, including the building of the terraces to accommodate the clerical offices, stables and servants' quarters.*

RIGHT: *The garden elevation of the William Gibbes residence, Charleston, South Carolina, USA, built in 1775. The ground floor, which is bypassed by curving stairs, is clearly of secondary importance.*

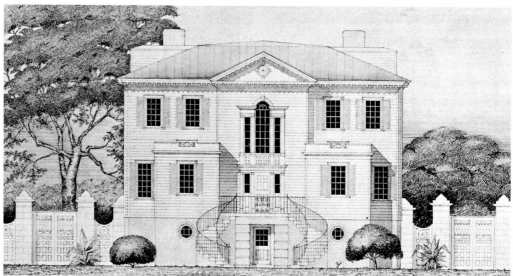

LEFT: *A Venetian or Palladian window at Mount Vernon, which was built in the 1770s for George Washington.*

RIGHT AND BOTTOM RIGHT: *Conventionally Classical columns, embellished with scrolls and acanthus leaves.*

BELOW: *A somewhat eccentric ornamentation of pillars.*

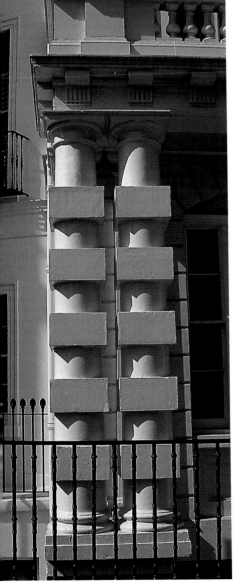

THIS PAGE: *Details of columns in Georgian buildings, showing elongated scrolls (top left), Ionic double-paired scrolls (bottom left), as at Kenwood House, north London, and the pared-down simplicity of the Tuscan order (below)*

of two-storeyed construction, the upper storey 'jettied', that is, projecting beyond the lower storey. Southern houses were usually one-storeyed and very simple in plan, having a central passageway to afford a through-draught in summer. Most houses were no more than one room deep under the main roof, although a lean-to or shed roof sometimes housed additional back rooms.

Imported Palladianism began to be manifest in the eastern cities by about 1740. Symmetrical façades, sash windows and external shutters became the order of the day, and brick was preferred to wood for the facing of individual elevations. Houses began to be grouped in terraces, as at London and Bath, first in Philadelphia from 1750. The new Palladian houses were at least two rooms deep. On the façades, the grander homes boasted Venetian (or Palladian) windows, pilasters and small, Classical porticoes to emphasise the entrance. Unlike their forerunners in Britain, American houses continued to have steeply pitched roofs with dormers, as had been particularly popular among

Dutch immigrants. This amalgam of styles proved both successful and durable for the houses of the well-to-do. The Palladian movement in America had its most pronounced impact on rural architecture.

Many of the ideas on which Georgian architecture was based were disseminated in America by British pattern books and materials, as well as by emigrant British designers, who worked both to existing models and to the instructions of the prospective owner; as in Britain, so too in the colonies, the chief architect of a great house was often the owner himself. What has been called 'the most beautiful town house in America', the Matthias Hammond house (1770) in Annapolis, Maryland, was designed by William Buckland, a craftsman from Oxford who was indentured for four years from 1755 to Thomas Mason as carpenter and joiner. Influence also came from sources other than British. 'Dutch colonial' houses, for example, with steep, double-pitched or gambrel (a form of mansard) roofs, were built

in numbers, and some still survive in New York and its district, reflecting the era when the city was a Dutch colony. Similarly, French settlers in Louisiana built houses that recalled those of their homeland or indeed those being built in the West Indies. These buildings usually featured a full-length porch and tall, floor-length windows.

The neo-Classical manner as expounded by the Adam brothers, which displaced Palladianism, was first seen in the American colonies in 1775 in George Washington's house at Mount Vernon. The lighter, more graceful style caught on, even in middle-class dwellings. Fanlights became more prominent, walls higher and roofs lower and no longer strewn with dormers and dominated by chimney stacks. The façade thus displayed a grid of symmetrically arranged, shuttered sash windows.

Immigration and independence in America combined to create a great diversity of house styles. Local vernacular models were re-created or adapted, with admixtures of imported features, making homes that were peculiar to their own region.

Thus Shaker houses in Kentucky used eighteenth-century façades fronting houses with starkly bare, minimalist interiors. In southern coastal towns, wooden-framed houses featured porches the length of each floor, the better to catch sea breezes.

Native architects were beginning to make their presence felt by 1800. The first great example was Thomas Jefferson, third President of the United States. Although his own designs were largely limited to grand projects, Jeffersonian Classicism, itself inspired directly by Palladio and by contemporary interpreters such as Buckland, had a profound impact on the development of the average home, a key distinguishing element being the Greek portico. Although design was becoming naturalised, however, supply was not, and America remained almost entirely dependent on Britain for furnishing and decorative materials until about 1825, when American manufacturers began to offer serious competition to imported goods.

OPPOSITE PAGE AND LEFT: *A selection of some of the many designs for capitals and modillions (ornamental brackets) available to architects from pattern books of the time, both in Great Britain and in America.*

LEFT: *With the improved production of glass, substantial glazing bars could be dispensed with, in favour of delicate wooden mouldings.*

BELOW AND LEFT: *Venetian windows and large bow windows are typical Georgian features.*

ABOVE: *The Window Tax, first imposed in 1696, was extended in 1766 to include all homes with seven or more windows, and in 1784 to homes with six or more. Owners accordingly bricked in some of the window openings to avoid paying the hated tax.*

Windows

The sash window was invented in perhaps 1670, and by 1720 was almost the only type of window opening used in all but remote country districts in both America and Britain until the early twentieth century. Well-suited to Classical architecture, the double-hung sash window became the quintessential window of the whole Georgian period.

The characteristic mid-Georgian window usually had twelve or sixteen panes (known in America as six-over-six or eight-

THIS PAGE: *Examples of windows, showing the diversity of designs. Pronounced bays were used in seaside towns to catch the sunlight radiating from the sea, but the bulging bow windows seen in modern mock-Georgian buildings never existed in Georgian times.*

ABOVE: *The east entrance façade of this house in Maine, USA, built in 1759, is faced with the wood-boarding that was used more commonly than stone or brick on the New England coast.*

RIGHT: *Beech Hill (now Hadley Golf Club House), built during the war years of 1793–1815 at the western edge of the then parish of Enfield, London. The four pilasters draw attention to the main entrance, which they frame.*

OPPOSITE PAGE: *A design for a window by Asher Benjamin (early nineteenth century). The scroll at the top is reminiscent of the Greek key design.*

over-eight windows). Later in the period windows generally became larger but had only eight or even four panes. Apron pieces, placed immediately below the window sills, were popular in the Georgian period in both plain and shaped forms. Occasionally these were replaced by recessed panels. Glazing bars typically became much more delicate than they had been up to the early eighteenth century.

By the early eighteenth century the Venetian or Palladian window, first used by Inigo Jones a century earlier, was common, even in less wealthy houses. The Venetian window had a central roundheaded section and two narrower side sections. A simpler variant consisted of a rectangular window with a central sash and two fixed lights at the side.

Domestic architecture of the mid-Georgian period (c.1760–1800) was dominated by the style of the Adam brothers, Robert and James. Under their influence, tripartite windows became fashionable, a wider light flanked by two narrower ones. The Venetian window was made more imposing by the use of an order of columns framing the lights. Favourite Adam devices were fan-filling, in which an outer arch echoing the inner arch over the central window and extending the width of the whole window enclosed a fan design; and a window with a pediment supported by consoles. A variation to the triple window was the semicircular window that was normally found in the middle of the top floor of a three-storeyed, double-fronted house.

From about the 1770s the first floor of the British town house was taking on the character of the *piano nobile* ('stately', or principal floor) and the windows were accordingly given the grand treatment, with external entablatures and giant columns (as at Royal Crescent, Bath) or pilasters extending up to the cornice. American houses, especially in the South, repeated this pattern. By the end of the eighteenth century, the *piano nobile* was a feature of most British houses, even terraced houses, which had either these tall windows or slightly shorter windows over small projecting balconies. Bow, or bay, windows, often extending almost the entire height of the external wall, were popular throughout the period. They admit more light than flat windows and were much used in seaside towns, where they could catch the sunlight reflecting off the sea. Elliptical and canted bays became popular at that time.

Georgian window glass has a slightly curved and ripply surface, very noticeable when it is viewed from one side. Its imperfections such as tiny air bubbles give it character and interest, and its beauty is enhanced by its sheen, its faint bluish or greenish tinge and its bell-like sound.

Towards the end of the Georgian period the production of larger and less vulnerable panes of glass wrought changes in window design. Heavy, substantial glazing bars could be dispensed with, in favour of delicate wooden mouldings in ogee, 'lamb's tongue' or 'Gothic' shapes. By the 1820s, when metal glazing bars were introduced, internal window supports became even fewer.

The existence of larger panes of glass gave rise to the French window and floor-length window, used particularly at the rear of a house to give onto a garden, verandah or conservatory. In the Regency period, narrow panes of glass, creating a border around the standard-sized panes and called margin lights, were often inserted in windows. Coloured glass – pink, blue, amber or lilac – was fashionable for the margin lights, as indeed for the principal panes. Sir John Soane's house in Lincoln's Inn Fields is suffused with a yellowish light from the amber glass which is used throughout.

THIS PAGE: *There are Classical references in all these doors. The most understated – top, centre – has panelling laid out in a way that echoes the sizes of windows in a Palladian house, the two tallest of six panels being in the centre and the two smallest at the top. Delicate patterns embellish the circular window and the fanlight in the door in the main picture.*

THIS PAGE: *Examples of Georgian doors. Pretty wrought ironwork frames the porch of the Regency door (top right).*

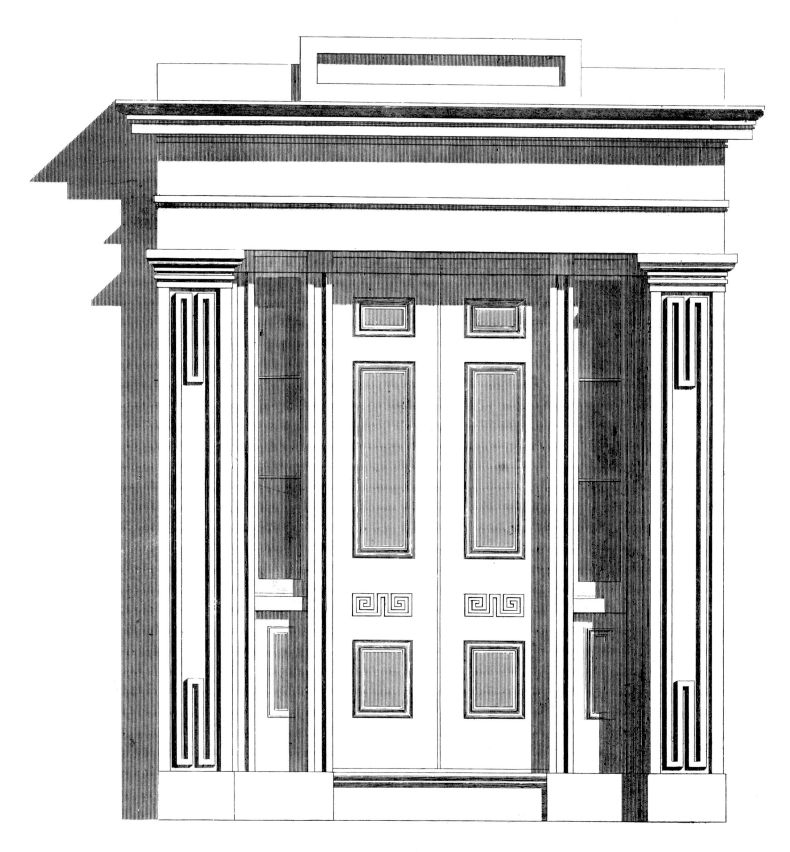

OPPOSITE PAGE: *Front door case design by Asher Benjamin, USA. The Greek key pattern was a favourite of his. Again, the panels echo the proportions of the façade windows.*

BELOW: *Design for a front door, also by Asher Benjamin, early nineteenth century.*

Doors and Door Furniture

In order to protect external doors from the weather and to emphasise their importance, they were often set within a porch or under a projecting upper storey. If not, they might be placed beneath a moulded projecting lintel. In stone houses, there might instead be drip mouldings across the tops of the doors. In the late Baroque period, these hoods and their brackets were highly ornamented. Hoods went out of fashion for a while until the late eighteenth century owing to the Georgians' preference for Palladian classicism, but when porches began to be thought inappropriate, they came back into style. Brackets and hoods were made of well seasoned softwood, usually carved and painted white. Pillars or pilasters sometimes supported the hoods, which were made in various shapes and sizes, including arches, coves and shell shapes and Classical triangular pediments in the temple front; or were 'aedicular' in style, with simple lintels, segmental, curved pediments and pagoda-style tops, a feature of the Regency period. The classical door surround, based first on Roman and later on Greek orders, constituted the popular 'tabernacle' frame, much favoured by the Adam brothers and generally preferred from the mid-eighteenth century.

On smaller town houses, doors were protected by nothing more than flat, moulded projections, though the supporting brackets were elaborately scrolled.

Until the nineteenth century, most door furniture was made of cast iron, painted black. Though brass rim locks were introduced in the late 1660s and brass handles fitted on some internal doors, replacing the older knobs, brass was generally too expensive a commodity for widespread use. The main item of door furniture common in the Georgian period was the door knob made of iron, plain and bold in design, and on front doors, set at waist height. Iron knockers were used on front doors, bearing all kinds of designs, usually based on animal heads. Door numbers became mandatory in London in 1805 but were affixed to the doors themselves only sporadically during the late Georgian period. Rim locks, which had knob and working parts set into a metal box mounted on the door and a latch that closed into a metal catch mounted on the door frame, began, in the mid-eighteenth century, to be replaced by mortise locks, the mechanism of which is covered by being sunk into the fabric of the door itself. These were usually made of iron, steel or brass. In 1784 Joseph Bramah invented a small, compact lock that was operated by the action of a rotating barrel, not a sliding bolt. This device was perfected with the development in the 1840s of the classic Yale cylindrical lock. The Chubb lock, a sophisticated mechanism that could detect tiny variations in key patterns, was patented in 1818. Hinges, made of wrought iron, could be of various types. Reproductions of Georgian hinges are poor substitutes for the originals, for which genuine replacements do not exist.

THIS PAGE AND OPPOSITE: *During the eighteenth century front door fittings were made of cast iron, painted black, and not of brass, which was an expensive commodity before the French Revolution. Front door knobs were usually centred at waist height, on the middle or lock rail. Letter boxes were a mid-Victorian addition. These items of door furniture are mostly modern reproduction;, however, any would be suitable for a genuine Georgian door.*

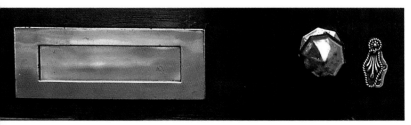

THIS PAGE: *A stone doorway to which the Roman Doric order has been applied and adapted.*

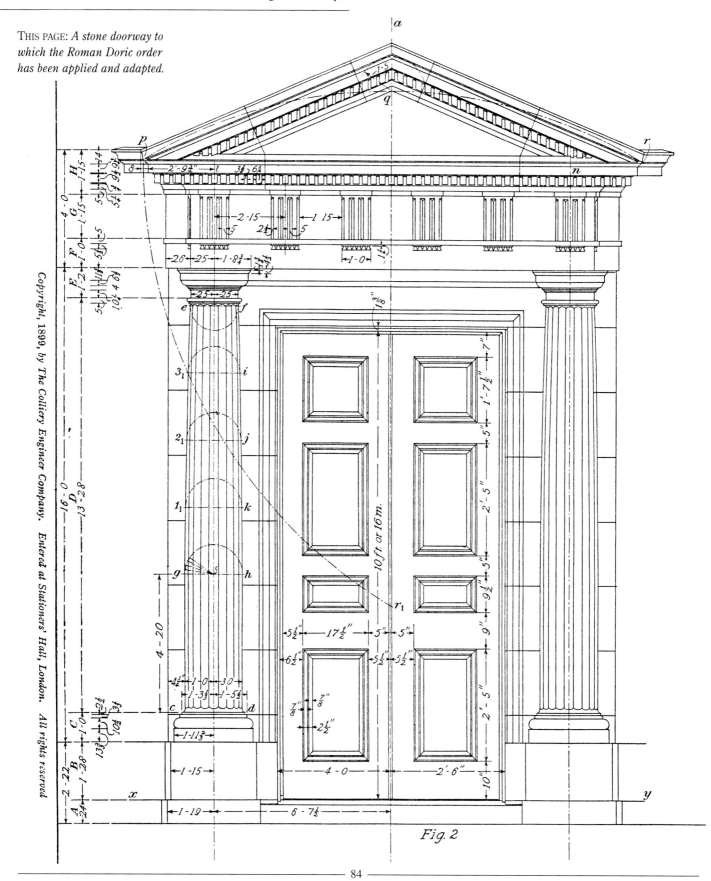

Fig. 2

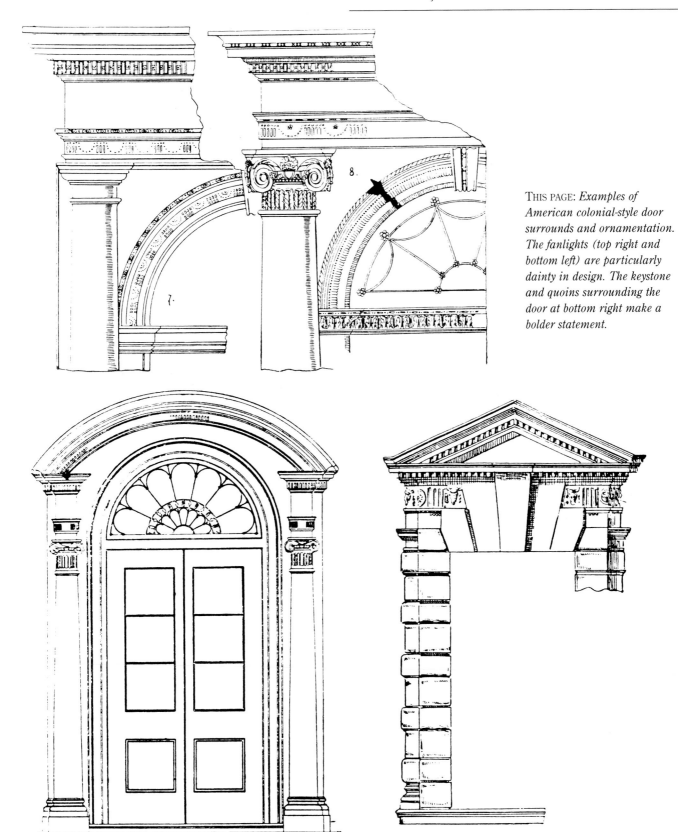

THIS PAGE: *Examples of American colonial-style door surrounds and ornamentation. The fanlights (top right and bottom left) are particularly dainty in design. The keystone and quoins surrounding the door at bottom right make a bolder statement.*

THIS PAGE: *Fanlights, which begin to appear in the 1720s and were popular until the 1840s, allowed light to enter the hall or corridor behind the front door and also provided the designer with scope for invention. The circular window (below) has a simple geometric pattern of leading. The other three examples show some intricate designs.*

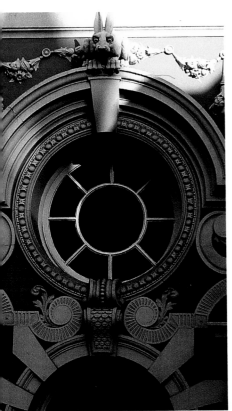

THIS PAGE: *Some unusual fanlights. Top left: an example with a more flamboyant, heavier-handed design. Centre left: a 'batswing' pattern, especially fashionable in the 1820s and 1830s, of essentially semicircular shape but set within a rectangular frame. Bottom left: a glass pane echoing the keystone shapes on the door arch. Below: a bold and imposing oval light.*

THIS PAGE: *Georgian fanlights of varying intricacy, dating probably from the 1760s and 1770s. These were large, complex compositions of iron and lead.*

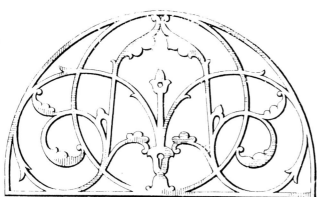

Fanlights

Glass fanlights over the front door first appeared in about the 1720s. They were functional, allowing light to enter the hall or corridor behind, and decorative, adding delight and individuality to the overall splendour of the façade. They were particularly liked among adherents of the elaborate and elegant Rococo and Adam styles. The front door made an important statement about the opulence of the house and the status of its owners. Fanlights reached the height of their popularity in Britain between about 1760 and 1780; in America, the peak was not until the 1780s, when the Adam-style fanlight became widely accepted. Glazing bars were made first of wood and then of lead or wrought iron.

In the Adam period fanlights were large and complex constructions increasingly made of cast iron, with delicate patterning extending across the whole width of the doorcase. By the end of the eighteenth century, fanlights were being mass-produced in a great variety of less formal designs, based on simple geometric shapes or serpentine curves. Loops and spider's webs replaced the earlier fans and scallops. Heart and honeysuckle motifs and 'teardrop' or 'batwing' designs were popular in the 1820s and 1830s. The use of such fanlights was widespread in terraces in cities and towns both in Britain and America. Early nineteenth-century fanlights were typically square or rectangular.

In 1832 good quality plate glass, known as 'broad' glass, was introduced, from which single-sheet lights could be made. These were structurally much stronger than traditional leaded lights, and did not need internal glazing bars, muntins (vertical framing pieces between panels) or leading. By the end of the Georgian period, builders were tending to insert glass into the body of the door itself, thus making fanlights superfluous. Many original fanlights were torn out by unsympathetic owners or developers in the early twentieth century. Replacements can still be obtained from craftworkers able to match designs to the age of the house.

Fanlights are usually better repaired than replaced with a modern reproduction. Some so-called 'Georgian' designs are poorly made copies. The glazing bars or leading should be integrated with the glass, and not stuck on the outside of it.

ABOVE: *Examples of English ironwork from the seventeenth and eighteenth centuries.*

RIGHT: *An elaborate fanlight with leading in the form of curves, swirls and flowers.*

ABOVE : *Adam-style grilles and fanlights, as illustrated by Joseph Bottomley, 1794.*

RIGHT: *A moulding in the form of a rosette, to be found on the ceiling of the porch at Kenwood House, London.*

BELOW: *A decorative convex moulding with a geometric and floral pattern which forms a balcony support.*

BELOW RIGHT: *Mouldings on a set of decorative arches in Regent's Park in London.*

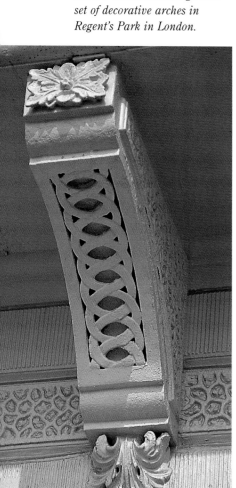

THIS PAGE: *Details of mouldings. In the Georgian period these might be made of stucco, wood or stone, and consisted of various designs: spirals, cups, sheaths, rosettes, animal heads, birds, reptiles, scrolls, egg-and-dart designs, griffins or chimerae.*

THIS PAGE AND OPPOSITE: *A selection of the many types of decorative mouldings to be found ornamenting Georgian buildings.*

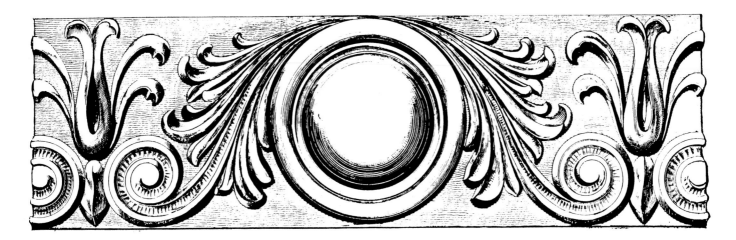

THIS PAGE: *Iron balconies were becoming increasingly common by the 1780s, replacing the familiar iron window-guards. They were normally cantilevered out from the first floor and supported both by brackets on their undersides and by iron beams that extended far into the house. Many balconies on existing Georgian buildings are painted black; the original colour would probably have been green. The balcony in the large picture (right) is a typically charming Regency example with the vaguely pagoda-shaped hood then in vogue.*

THIS PAGE: *Balconies might also have stone balustrades or demonstrate hybrid forms, combining Classical styles such as columns and pilasters with Georgian-period ironwork.*

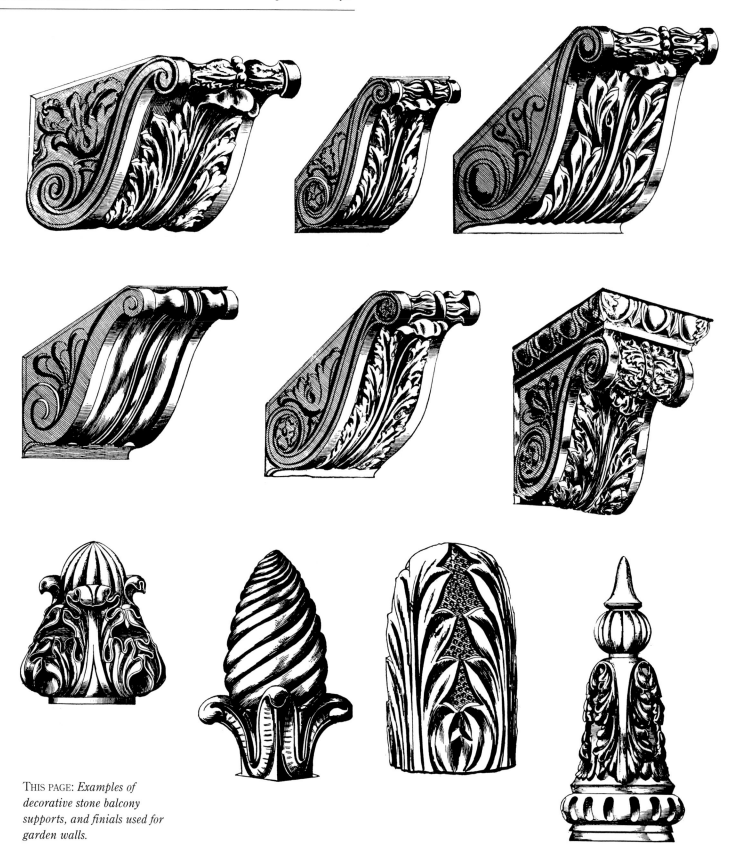

THIS PAGE: *Examples of decorative stone balcony supports, and finials used for garden walls.*

THIS PAGE: *Crestings such as these would be found decorating the apex of a roof or, made of cast iron, as ornamentation added to window-sills.*

THIS PAGE: *A variety of Georgian roofs and pediments. Tiles began to be superseded by slates, which permitted shallower roof pitches than tiles and were more efficient at keeping out rain. Diminishing courses of slates, as in the example at bottom left, were laid to transfer the bulk of the weight of the roof covering to the outer walls. It was fashionable to hide the roof itself from view at street level, by placing the roof-line parallel to a high, street-front parapet, as in some of the examples here (top left and right, and centre).*

THIS PAGE: *Roofs, showing some of the bulky chimneys, prominent dormer windows, onion domes and turrets and high parapets that were typical of the period. Many Georgian houses had M-shaped (double-pitched) roofs with valley gutters. Mansard roofs were also common. The roof at bottom right is an example of Georgian Gothick, an exuberant interpretation of Gothic style that came to prominence in the 1820s.*

BELOW: *Two designs for ironwork lamp brackets, by the Adam brothers, for Drapers' Hall, London.*

ABOVE: *Three examples of ironwork brackets used to support shelters to doorways.*

RIGHT: *Designs for ironwork lamp-holders, such as may be seen outside No.10 Downing Street, London. These were published by Carter in 1750.*

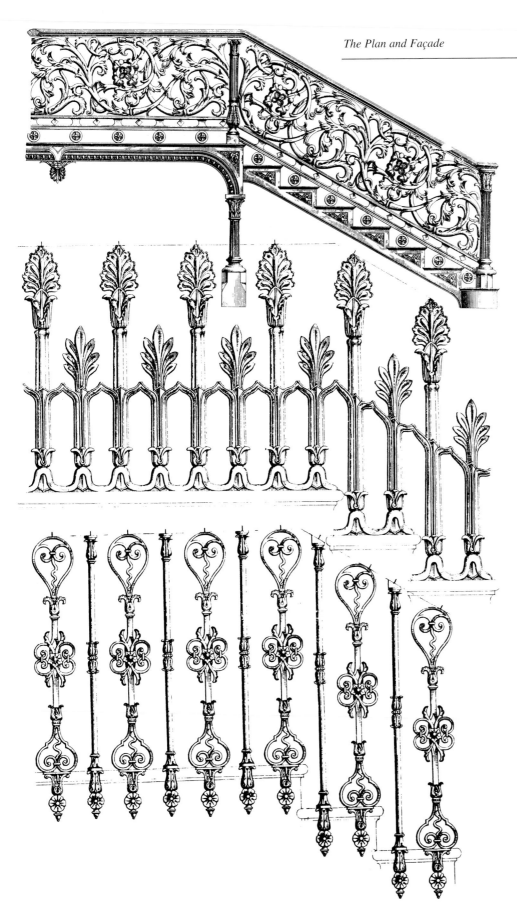

THIS PAGE: *Cast- or wrought-iron balusters were becoming very common by 1800. Some might support a rail of mahogany. Decorative elements might be made of cast brass or lead. These examples are all open-string staircases, where the treads have been left exposed (sometimes, as in the example at the top of the page, elegantly carved). Where the balusters consisted of posts, these were often placed two, or even three to a stair.*

THIS PAGE: *Examples of drainpipes, gutters and rainwater heads. Until about the end of the eighteenth century, these were made of softwood, sometimes lined with lead. Many later examples were made from cast iron. Lead was another commonly used roofing material.*

THIS PAGE: *Iron boot-scrapers in various shapes and sizes, notably the lyre-shaped example (bottom, second from left).*

THIS PAGE: *Early Georgian railings consisted of massive uprights terminating in spiked finials in the form of weapon heads. Through the eighteenth century, railings became more complex, lighter and more elaborately patterned (the patterns sometimes made of stamped or cast lead). Heart and honeysuckle (the classically derived anthemion) motifs were popularised by the Adam brothers. The examples at the top are from Great Ormond Street, London, and include a boot-scraper and a lamp support.*

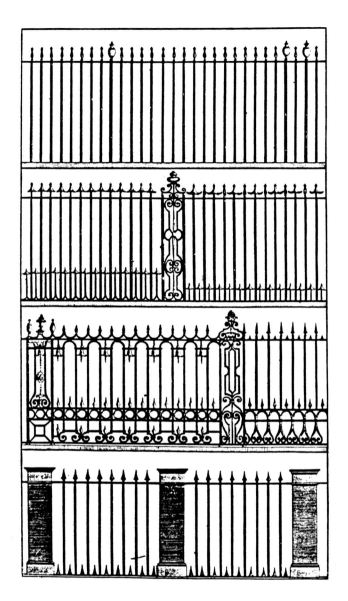

ABOVE: *A balcony railing from an American house built in 1811 by George Hyde Clark.*

LEFT: *Railings designed by Isaac Ware, 1756.*

BELOW AND BOTTOM: *Further examples of English ironwork. Those below right are described as 'lyre railing pilasters'.*

THIS PAGE: *Georgian ironwork in both functional and decorative guises. The white-painted motif occupying the shaft of a column (centre right) is to be seen at Kenwood House, north London.*

THIS PAGE: *More Georgian ironwork, including lamp holders, gates and gate posts, railings and finials.*

RIGHT: *Design for an iron gate, from James Gibbs's* Book of Architecture, *1728.*

BELOW: *A wrought-iron gate from Westover, Virginia in the USA, 1726.*

LEFT: *Wrought-iron gates such as the example shown here were very fashionable for the grander Georgian houses.*

BELOW LEFT: *Garden gates at Scraptoft Hall, near Leicester, designed by William Edney. The design features a large central rosette and a scroll pattern repeating four times; at the sides are pilasters with lyre-motif fillings.*

BELOW: *A railing by Robert Adam in St James's Square, London, 1773. The verticals finish in mace heads and the ornamentation consists of* fleur-de-lis *and honeysuckle borders.*

BOTTOM: *Balustrade to the Strand front of Somerset House, London, probably designed by Sir William Chambers and erected in or after 1776. It consists of eight rather massive panels of scrolls with fan-shaped centres between stone pillars.*

Chapter 3
Interiors
and Furnishings

*'Perhaps there is not a thing upon the face of the earth truer than
the belief that taste is the general possession of all men;
I mean every man assumes it to himself, tho' he denies it to his
neighbour, by which it is at once universal in one view,
and non-existent in another.'*

*John Shebbeare ('Battista Angeloni') (1709–88), letter to the Reverend Father Filippo
Bonini in Rome, 1755, from* Letters on the English Nation

OPPOSITE PAGE: *The eighteenth-
century dining room at
Hatchlands, Surrey, is full of
typical Robert Adam features,
notably the ceiling and chimney
breast ornament. He carried
out the interior decoration in
1759 and it is his earliest
known work in England.*

BELOW: *A detail of the Adam
chimneypiece in the dining
room at Hatchlands.*

From medieval times, the lord of the manor and the ladies of the household had been accorded a certain amount of privacy, even in the grimmest of castles. 'Solars' or parlours were rooms for each to relax, sew, chat with friends, sing or play musical instruments. Private sitting rooms and individual bedrooms continued to be the standard arrangement into the Tudor period and beyond. The servants were relegated to garrets and attics, and the hall – once such a vital component of English homes – fell into disuse except as a place where large numbers of people could dine together, although the family ate apart. Gradually the servants acquired their own self-contained quarters, and the hall was left for ceremonial purposes only. In smaller houses, private rooms were usually fairly small, with low ceilings and dark panelling – possibly advantages in bedrooms, where warmth and snugness were desirable.

In the 'prodigy houses' of the seventeenth century – stately homes that have been since so designated because they were fine, innovative and impressive – increasing importance was given to private family life, and accordingly such houses were provided with summer and winter parlours and with two-room suites, known as 'lodgings', allotted to each member of the

family. A long gallery, a prestige room inherited from earlier building traditions, was perpetuated and used for the taking of exercise, indoor games and the making of music. It was usually sited on the first floor. Where the ground level had once been the only floor with any status, upper-floor rooms now began to gain in importance, and with them the staircase, which was no longer hidden away or neglected but became a feature worthy of display. Fireplaces, too, came out into the open and became the focus of decorative treatment with a carved and panelled surround. The main reception rooms, however, continued to be on the ground floor.

By the later seventeenth century, it had become fashionable to entertain dinner guests in the French manner, at several small tables rather than at a single large one, although the family still ate in their own private dining room. Kitchens, hitherto on the ground floor, now began to be moved down to a basement or semi-basement. In all but the largest houses, a preference was growing for smaller, intimate and more comfortable apartments. The long string of rooms that opened into each other, without corridors or passages, and that had often grown, 'Topsy'-like, in a fairly random manner, gave way to a compact, box-like plan, with backstairs and passages.

With the introduction of the Palladian style, the most important reception rooms of larger houses and villas were placed not at ground level but on the first floor – the *piano nobile* ('stately storey'). For practical as well as decorative reasons, imposing porticoes were built with flights of steps leading up to the first floor, which was where the main entrance hall

RIGHT AND OPPOSITE PAGE: *Two chinoiserie designs for interiors by William Chambers (1723–96). He was born in Sweden of Scottish descent and had, unlike most of his contemporaries, actually visited China, where he became inspired by the Chinese style. Chinoiserie became very fashionable and was adopted by other architects and designers who also used it for furniture and whole buildings. It featured, for example, balconies covered by roofs of copper or lead, in emulation of the curved roof-line of a Chinese pagoda.*

was now usually situated. The excessive formality of strict Palladian design precluded the intrusion into the entrance hall of the main staircase, which might disrupt the symmetry, and it was therefore tucked away behind or to one side, in an inner hall.

In Palladian houses, too, and in some of their successors, comfort and convenience were secondary to the achievement of gracious, perfect architectural proportions. The kitchens, for example, were often placed in wings or pavilions detached from, and a long distance from, the main block of the house and reached only by covered ways, underground passages or even open courtyards. 'There is no doubt,' historian Michael I. Wilson has written (*The English Country House and its Furnishings*, London, Batsford, 1977), 'that much of the hot food intended for

our ancestors was tepid before it reached the table; yet equally there is no doubt that such small inconveniences were philosophically endured in the cause of art.' At Heveningham Hall, Suffolk, designed c.1778 by Sir Robert Taylor, the original plans provided for a library at the east end of the gallery, a drawing room against most of its north wall, and beyond that (with a screened end corresponding with the screened end of the gallery, and communicating with it) an eating room.

A worse disposition cannot possibly be imagined. Of course, this eating room was only for ceremonious occasions, the family habitually taking its meals in the common dining room ... But to serve into the eating room meant a procession of dishes passing

from the kitchen, along the back passage, through the great hall, into the ante-chamber, along the gallery, and then, at last, into the room where they were to be consumed... [A later disposition was] just a little better, as the food reached its haven after passing across the hall only.

(H. Avray Tipping, *English Homes: Period VI– Vol. I, Late Georgian, 1760–1820*, London, *Country Life*, 1926).

Also for aesthetic reasons, it was thought appropriate that the main bedrooms should be on the same floor as, and interconnected with, the reception rooms, even though this arrangement actually afforded less domestic privacy than had been attained in the preceding era, and was in that sense something of a retrogression.

Reception rooms were used for different purposes – dancing, gambling, eating and playing cards. The saloon was a large room

OPPOSITE PAGE: *The library fireplace at Hatchlands, Surrey (1758–61) includes round medallions and bas-reliefs of classical figures typical of Robert Adam's designs.*

LEFT: *This striking fireplace with its dominant Greek key design is further decorated with* Bossi *work – the technique of carving out white marble and infilling with decorative, coloured marble. Bartoli, an Italian craftsman of the period, was a master of this technique, and Robert Adam used his skills on a number of fireplaces.*

in the bigger houses for entertaining on a grand scale. It was designed along the lines of the French salon as a setting for the finer cultural and social pursuits. Doubtless such a refined atmosphere did sometimes prevail. Equally, there would have been occasions that resembled Lord Hervey's description (in a letter to Horace Walpole in 1776) of a court gathering: '... last night there was dice, dancing, crowding, sweating and stinking in abundance.' One popular leisure activity was the drinking of tea, a habit that, once begun in the 1660s, had become the rage among the upper strata of society, the only clientele who could readily afford it. Since it was so expensive, the tea was made in the saloon, or sometimes in the drawing room, by the mistress of the house herself. A servant would bring in a tea caddy – locked against unscrupulous would-be traders or those who merely aspired to indulge in this luxury – and then the water would be heated in a silver kettle suspended on a stand over a spirit lamp. The popularity of tea-drinking led to the introduction of tea caddies, containers, pots, cups, kettle stands and tea tables, all turned out with great care.

Since 1660 it had become increasingly important for all but the most modest houses to have a library. The Palladian movement and the custom of taking the Grand Tour went hand in hand with a desire for classical learning, and where this was not genuine it was usually assumed for the purposes of show.

Status was to be had in owning a library, even if it was filled with never-opened volumes or even dummy book-backs.

In the early Georgian period, the dining room was used for dining only. The dining table, incidentally, was not always kept in it but sometimes outside in a passage or corridor, to be brought in when a meal was about to be served. The tables were consequently plain and had drop leaves to facilitate storage. Later, the function of the dining room widened. After dinner it was used by the men for conversation. Robert Adam, the great interior designer of the mid-Georgian period, believed that some of the most significant political and social decisions were made by gentlemen sitting over their port after meals. He accordingly gave considerable attention to the accoutrements of port-drinking: an ornamental sideboard with a marble top, wine-coolers, cutlery containers, plate racks, lamps for warming plates and lead-lined tanks for the rinsing of the glasses and cutlery, some of these housed in free-standing urns on pedestals.

During the eighteenth century, the drawing room in better households became the focus of the house. It had its origins in the sixteenth century as a private room for 'withdrawing' to after a big social event. Increasingly it became larger and friendlier to the presence of visitors, so that by the mid-eighteenth century it had blossomed into the principal reception room. It still also served, however, as a place of refuge from the hurly-burly of

OPPOSITE PAGE: *Design for a late Georgian living room. Typical motifs were the swags below the ceiling cornice and above the door and the lyre shape in the chair backs. The furniture was probably of mahogany.*

ABOVE: *An early Georgian living room with an alcove, in which stand a dresser and a writing table and chair.*

LEFT: *A room designed by the architect Thomas Hope in 1807; it is described as 'in the Classic style', but represents the fashion for the Egyptian that was at its height between 1804 and 1810, probably as a result of Napoleon's Egyptian campaign. Even the chair arm-rests feature human figures in the appropriate style.*

RIGHT: *Marble-topped tables grace this opulent room, lit by an elaborate chandelier.*

BELOW: *An elegant chimneypiece with fluted pilasters at the sides is a prominent feature of this room.*

LEFT: *The deep colour of the walls in this room at Hatchlands, Surrey, was typical of Georgian tastes. The house was built in 1756 by Admiral Boscawen, who defeated the French fleet at Louisberg in 1758. The fireplace is an original by Robert Adam.*

formal entertaining, where women retired to take tea and gossip. As well as being the best-appointed room in the house, it was also the airiest, the most comfortable and the lightest, with the longest and widest windows, sometimes giving access to a verandah. At the opposite end from the windows, mahogany double doors might give on to the dining room.

By about 1800, the disregard for convenience that had characterised Palladian houses had largely crumbled in the face of common sense. The dining room, and sometimes the drawing room too, had slipped down a floor from the *piano nobile* to ground level, where there was better access to and from the main entrance and to the kitchen, which, in the great houses of Britain and America, might be in the core area of the house or, if not, then in an adjacent wing or subsidiary building. In the typical terraced house of the Georgian period, the kitchen was always on the ground floor, in the basement or, if the house had a large rear yard, in a separate structure there.

The parlour, which in middle-class homes complemented the drawing room and in poorer homes was a substitute for it, also acquired a different role as the eighteenth century progressed, becoming more and more a private room to which the family could retire.

A noticeable feature of house-planning after 1750 was the provision of a music room or apartment, a response to the growing popularity of private concert-giving. Before then, music had been performed in the hall, the long gallery or in a private parlour. By the Regency period, dining rooms and drawing rooms were (still) on the ground floor of larger houses, often opening out at each side of the entrance hall, but new types of room had begun to appear frequently: the morning room, the study and the billiards room. The kitchen (sometimes together with washhouse, bakehouse and scullery) was at the back of the house, while bedrooms of family and staff were on the upper floor or floors, to which servants had their own staircase. If this arrangement seems familiar to a twentieth-century reader, it is because it foreshadows that of modern houses.

RIGHT: *A page from George Hepplewhite's* The Cabinet Maker and Upholsterer's Guide *showing a plan of a room and the 'proper' distribution of its furniture; dating from the 1790s.*

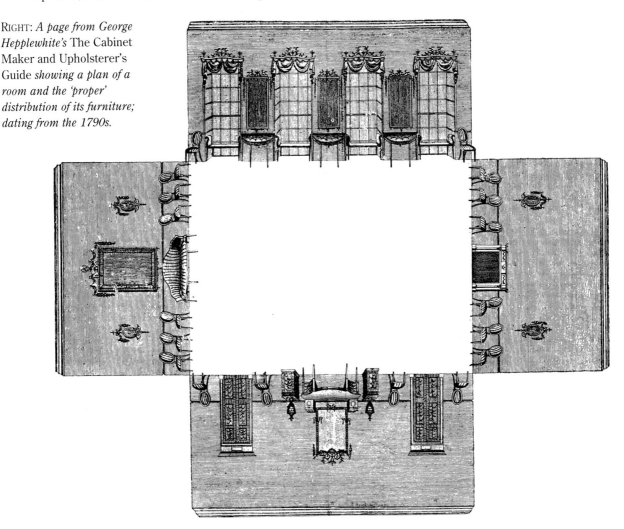

LEFT: *A sideboard designed by Thomas Sheraton, 1793. The vase-like containers on the ends are knife-holders.*

BELOW: *Dining-room furniture designed by Robert Adam, at Harewood House, Yorkshire. The house was built between 1759 and 1771 by John Carr of York for Edwin Lascelles, whose heir became the 1st Earl of Harewood. Robert Adam was responsible for the decoration of the house interior.*

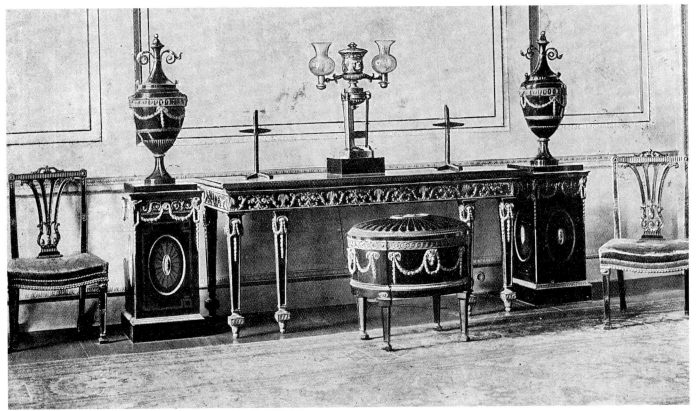

RIGHT: *A living room with a fine chimneypiece with a pine and marble surround and a brass fire-basket.*

BELOW: *The room of Mrs Fitzherbert (with whom George IV contracted a secret and invalid marriage in December 1785) at the Royal Pavilion, Brighton, Sussex.*

OPPOSITE PAGE: *The designs of the wallpaper and furniture give this elegant dining room the feel of the chinoiserie style, popular in Georgian England.*

RIGHT: A *mahogany sideboard
with an inlay of satinwood,
designed by Robert Adam
(probably 1760s–1770s). The
vases would have held cutlery.*

Furniture

Behind the dignified, somewhat austere elegance of the Palladian house exterior, decorations and furnishings of great richness and exuberance were commonly to be found. In the grander house setting, the influence of William Kent was enormous. Chairs, tables and settees designed by him had scroll-like legs, with huge swags and loops of fruit, flowers or leaves hung between them, all carved in wood or modelled in plaster and then gilded or painted white or both. Chair-arm terminals sported masks of satyrs and goddesses. Console tables rested on the outstretched wings of eagles. Such magnificent if ponderous design inevitably lost some of its panache as it filtered down through the classes to ordinary households, where it had its greatest impact on ornamental rather than functional items, such as side tables, mirror frames and candlestands – portable platforms carrying single or branched candlesticks or perfume burners. Side tables were found in most rooms of importance in Palladian mansions, almost all ornamental and topped by massive slabs of marble or scagliola (imitation marble). These were often described as console tables, a term that strictly denotes tables having front legs only and screwed at the back to the wall. Many of these floridly decorated, bulky tables were designed with a large mirror to match.

While the Palladian movement was at its height in the 1720s and 1730s, and indeed for the whole of the first half of the eighteenth century, the design and ornamentation of furniture were essentially the province of architects. Large pieces especially – bureaux, bookcases and cabinets, for example – received the Classical treatment, their plain surfaces being embellished with pilasters and half-columns, mouldings and friezes and most of the other motifs and devices that were customarily seen on the buildings themselves. Walnut had been the standard wood used for furniture even before the Georgian period, but by the late 1730s it had been long overtaken by mahogany imported from Spanish South America (since the lifting in 1721 of duty on timber imported from the North American colonies and the West Indies). Mahogany had a rich, dark red colour that was much admired, it did not crack or warp, it readily accepted carving and it was stronger, more durable and more resistant to woodworm than walnut. Spanish mahogany, on the other hand, was expensive and so began to be used principally as a veneer, although legs of furniture continued to be made in the solid. Later in the century Honduras mahogany, a wood lighter in colour and weight, was introduced.

Chairs of 1720–5 were typically slightly curved, with vaguely vase-shaped backs and somewhat concave sides. Thereafter, by about 1740, seats and backs tended to become square again, as in the late seventeenth century, but nearly all examples of chairs from these two decades displayed cabriole ('goat's-leap') legs and claw-and-ball feet (representing the claws of a dragon, bird of prey or lion). This style was applied also to the legs and feet of settees, armchairs and tables.

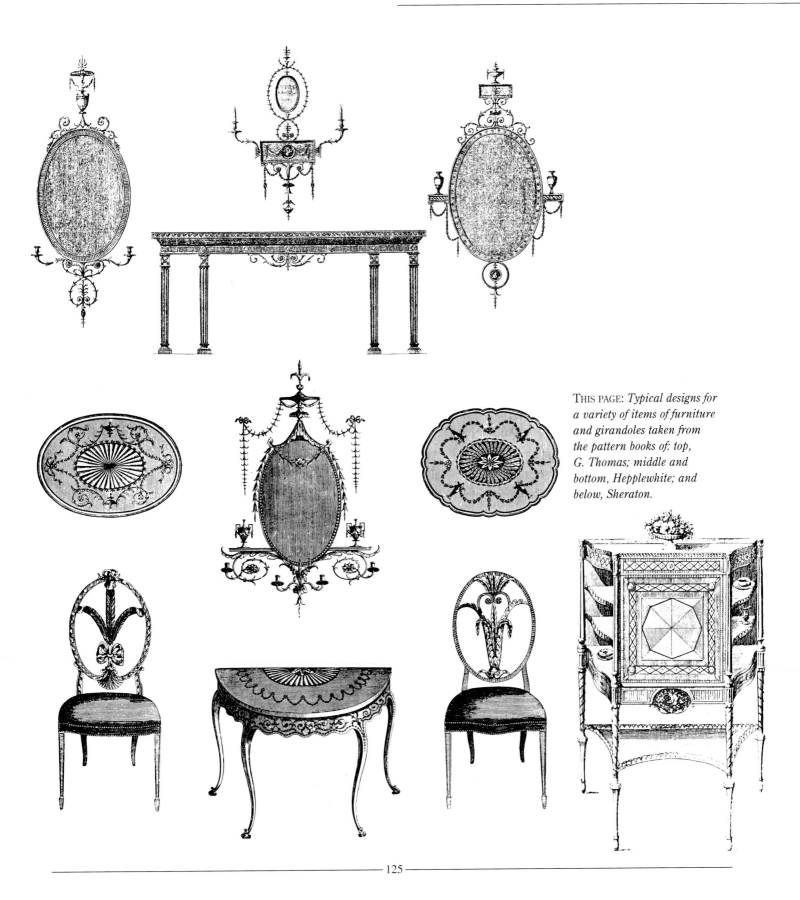

THIS PAGE: *Typical designs for a variety of items of furniture and girandoles taken from the pattern books of: top, G. Thomas; middle and bottom, Hepplewhite; and below, Sheraton.*

Dining tables had flaps supported on swing legs, on the gate-leg principle. The tables were at first usually oval; later, rectangular tables that could be pushed together to form a continuous long surface became popular. Folding gaming tables were often beautifully crafted. Most of these were square and there were various mechanisms by which they could be opened out, some more aesthetically pleasing than others.

By the 1740s the new spirit of the age was the then so-called 'French taste', now retrospectively known as Rococo, a style distinguished by its deliberate asymmetry and its floridity of carving, especially in scroll shapes. Such characteristics were aptly applied to girandoles (ornamental wall lights, having one or more candle branches and often a mirror, too) and other ornamental pieces, less so to functional items such as chairs and tables. From then on, 'judgement in the materials, ... taste in the fashions, and skill in the workmanship' (according to the author of *The London Tradesman*, 1747) were most profoundly moulded by Thomas Chippendale (1718–79), cabinet-maker and upholsterer and author of the famous *The Gentleman and Cabinet-Maker's Director* (1754). The pieces of furniture that can be reliably attributed to Chippendale himself are as few as the items that reflect his influence between about 1750 and 1780 are many. His *Director* was the most comprehensive of numerous pattern books published from the 1740s onwards, and the first to be devoted to furniture alone. Chippendale-style

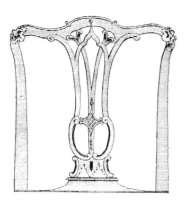

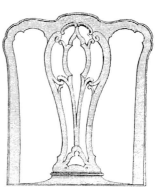
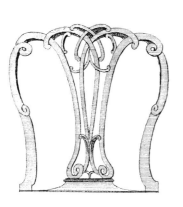

furniture is generally associated with soberness of design, although the original designs in the *Director* are more flamboyant, and richer in ornamental carving, a feature that Chippendale himself recognised as an optional extra, which could 'be left out, if desired'. Chippendale-style chairs were marked by square rather than rounded seats and backs, cupid's-bow back tops and a central back upright (the 'splat') of carved openwork. Some continued to have cabriole legs and claw-and-ball feet – others plain, straight legs and curl or scroll feet. The *Director* included also what its author called 'French chairs' – armchairs, stuffed not sprung. In a letter to Sir Edward Knatchbull at Mersham le Hatch, Kent, in May 1773, Chippendale recommended:

2 large Berjairs [bergères] as we think it would be of more propriety in one room – as the Chairs can only at present be finished in Linnen We should be glad to know what kind of Covers You would please to have for them – Serge is most commonly us'd but as the room is hung with India paper you might Chuse some sort of Cotton – suppose a green stripe Cotton which at this is fashionable –.

The *Director* devoted considerable space to library furniture. The traditional architectural designs for bookcases and bureaux were retained, though softened by flowing shapes and enlivened by Rococo carving. The so-called 'cockfighting' chair of the period was intended in fact for use in a library; it had a small desk attached to the back so that the reader, having turned around, could use the chair as a stool and the incurving rail of the back as supports for the elbows. The typical Chippendale desk consisted of two pedestals containing drawers and separated by

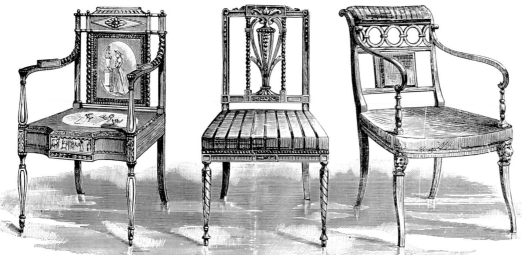

OPPOSITE PAGE, TOP: *A modern-day reproduction of a Hepplewhite urn-back chair, c.1780s.* BYLAW THE FURNITURE MAKERS

OPPOSITE PAGE, BOTTOM: *Chair-back designs by Thomas Chippendale. The central splat of carved openwork was a favourite with Chippendale.*

THIS PAGE: *Furniture design by Thomas Sheraton, c.1793. Sheraton was especially fond of the square-backed chair with a straight, horizontal top.*

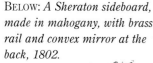

BELOW: *A Sheraton sideboard, made in mahogany, with brass rail and convex mirror at the back, 1802.*

BOTTOM: *A 'sofa table' design by Thomas Sheraton, 1804. This type of table, which had a flap at each end, was used as a writing table from c.1790.*

BELOW: *A bookcase design by Thomas Chippendale, 1759.*

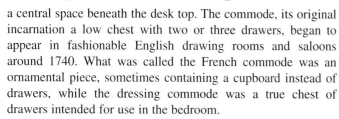

a central space beneath the desk top. The commode, its original incarnation a low chest with two or three drawers, began to appear in fashionable English drawing rooms and saloons around 1740. What was called the French commode was an ornamental piece, sometimes containing a cupboard instead of drawers, while the dressing commode was a true chest of drawers intended for use in the bedroom.

Chippendale's was also influential in promulgating the Chinese taste that became known as chinoiserie. Furniture in this style typically displayed a sharply angular lattice or trellis pattern. Little carved bells and angular peaks suggestive of pagodas were nearly always to be found, too. Chinese designs appeared on chairs, couches, tables and cabinets, as indeed on balustrades and other fixtures. At Padworth House, Berkshire, a mahogany settee (1765) has legs and frame in the Chinese manner, and coverings in needlework illustrating biblical and mythological subjects; chairs have legs enriched with a Chinese fret and a covering of floral needlework on an indigo blue ground. To accompany the Chinese décor, oriental dinner sets were imported from China through the East India Company

during the eighteenth century, and were especially favoured by rich city merchants with country seats, for example Sir William Baker of Bayfordbury, Hertfordshire. Where originals could not be afforded, chinoiserie imitations were substituted.

Incidentally, Chippendale was not always stationed at his premises in St Martin's Lane but went travelling to his clients in, for example, Yorkshire and Kent, giving estimates for complete furnishings and decoration. As well as supplying the most exquisite pieces of reception-room furniture, he also offered household utensils such as carpet brooms and feather brushes.

The Gothick craze developed from about the 1760s. In furniture its presence is always recognisable by a pointed-arch device, in any of its variations (such as the ogee arch) and in almost any position. During this period, a wondrous confusion between Gothick and chinoiserie reigned, such that pieces were produced that combined the two or, if nominally distinct, were barely to be differentiated. Gothick tables, chairs and cabinets resemble their Chinese-style counterparts in having no feet on their straight legs, often bearing fretwork in trellis-like patterns and in having similar cluster-column legs, here inspired not by

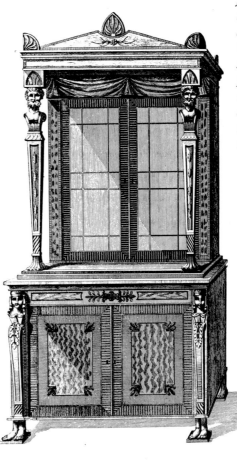

THIS PAGE: *Large pieces of furniture such as these bookcases by Adam (far left) and Sheraton (left) received the Classical treatment, their plain surfaces being embellished with pilasters and half-columns, mouldings and friezes and most of the other motifs and devices that were customarily seen on the buildings themselves.*

bundles of bamboo but by stone-and-marble medieval pillars.

As in the exteriors of buildings, so too in their interiors and furnishing, English style was revolutionised by the arrival on the scene in the 1760s and early 1770s of Robert Adam and his brothers, who did away with the heavy Palladian mode and replaced it with a light and delicate style of decoration. At Osterley Park, Hounslow, Middlesex, where Adam was at work for almost twenty years from 1761, he produced beechwood armchairs with cane seats and painted with 'Etruscan' ornament (1776), perhaps among the earliest surviving painted armchairs. The back splat is in the shape of a Greek vase. Similarly the Greek lyre shape appeared on his eating-room and library chair backs. Adam chairs and tables both have delicately tapered round or square legs, peg or spade feet, fluting (grooves) or reeding (convex strips) and ornament in the form of a Greek patera – an oval, or round decoration, carved, inlaid or painted on. Notable among other pieces of Adam furniture are oval-backed armchairs with rounded seats, dining-room sideboards, flap tables that could be set together for dining, wall furniture such as mirrors, side tables and commodes, semi-ornamental

pieces such as pedestals and candlestands (often tripod-shaped), gilt-metal lamps and hanging lanterns, and rectangular, later semicircular commodes. A dining-room side table in mahogany, dating from about 1770, at Padworth House, has an enriched patera Adam motif used very unusually in halves and quarters as a valance to the table frame.

Incidentally, the backs of chairs and other pieces of living-room furniture were often quite plain because in the more public rooms it was customary to range the furniture round the walls until it was moved forwards, probably by a servant, for use. This practice, which made the principal reception rooms look rather like parade-grounds, suddenly disappeared after 1800, when the modern habit of dotting furniture around in the middle of the room took over, perhaps as a result of changing ladies' fashions. A lady draped in the Grecian-style robe that was in vogue during the Regency could move more easily between pieces of furniture than her mother or grandmother had been able to do while wearing the full skirts popular in the mid-eighteenth century. She was also more able to recline and was thus more likely to be seen draped over a sofa instead of sitting stiffly in a chair.

Thomas Chippendale and other cabinet-makers assimilated and drew on Adam's style in their actual making of pieces of furniture. Even when the Adams' fame and success had begun to decline, their style was perpetuated, in a more populist form, and adapted to the pockets of the less wealthy, by George Hepplewhite (fl. 1760–86) and Thomas Sheraton (1751–1806). Hepplewhite's *The Cabinet Maker and Upholsterer's Guide* (1788, later editions in 1789 and 1794) gave designs for smart but serviceable furniture, including his trademark, the shield-back chair decorated with the Prince of Wales's feathers (three ostrich plumes arranged in the form of a crown). Other Adam motifs and designs were retained, with the exception of the stuffiest Classical elements. Hepplewhite deigned, as Adam had not done, to present designs for mundane items such as washstands, chests of drawers and occasional tables, notably the Pembroke, which had a falling flap along each side and often a small drawer.

Sheraton's best known work was *The Cabinet Maker and Upholsterer's Drawing Book*, published in four parts between 1791 and 1794. Sheraton was particularly fond of the square-backed chair with a straight, horizontal top. His designs were, on the whole, in the Adam manner, though perhaps displaying a French-inspired elegance that does not so pervade the work of Hepplewhite. Sheraton also promoted the idea of painted ornament applied to furniture. Other books of design were abroad at the time, notably *The Cabinet-Maker's London Book of Prices* (1788) by Thomas Shearer which is distinguished by a number of designs for functional pieces such as secretaires, washstands and dressing tables.

The succeeding Regency period was typified by restraint, with notable exceptions such as the extreme Orientalism of Sezincote, Gloucestershire, built c.1803 in the Indian style, and the Royal Pavilion, Brighton (remodelled c.1801). The Regency house generally contained furniture that already had a pedigree, such as the Pembroke table, as well as the latest in both items and designs. The sofa table was a Regency innovation that became almost a necessity in any house, serving as a side table in grander homes and doing duty in lesser households as a dining table. It was rectangular in shape, had flaps along its short side, often had two drawers and moved about on brass castors, sometimes concealed in a modelled lion's paw. The sofa table was originally intended to be used in association with a sofa, itself a low-backed, scrolled-end item perfectly suited to languid relaxation. Sofa, sofa table and chairs usually stood on legs with a concave curve reminiscent of a sabre or scimitar, a shape derived from classical Greece, although in the circumstances of the Napoleonic wars, Trafalgar and the death of Nelson, admirably appropriate to the military mood of the time. Chairs typically feature sabre-shaped legs, fairly high arms with scrolled ends, low, square backs and scrolled back uprights. The more opulent models were painted and gilded.

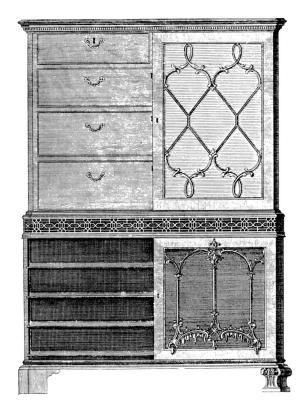

OPPOSITE PAGE AND FAR LEFT, TOP AND BOTTOM: *Sofas and cabinets from Chippendale's* The Gentleman and Cabinet-Maker's Director *(1754). His* Director *was the most comprehensive of numerous pattern books published from the 1740s onwards, and the first to be devoted to furniture alone.*

LEFT: *A French marquetry-work secretaire with plaques of Sèvres porcelain and ormolu mounts from the mid-eighteenth century.*

BELOW: *A glazed bookcase with fluted pilasters. This handmade reproduction cabinet strives to emulate the ethos of the period.*
BYLAW THE FURNITURE MAKERS

A carved moulding resembling rope was affixed to some chairs, hence called 'Trafalgar' chairs, and other naval motifs – anchors, dolphins – were common.

In wealthy households the side table with flanking pedestals and rail at the back to support plates was popular. Less fashionable and thus more common in modest houses was the chiffonier, originally a French clothes cupboard with double doors and a back frame fitted with a shelf surmounting the top. Sideboards, chiffoniers, chairs and other furniture were often decorated, after about 1815, with inlaid strips of brass, or with boulle, an form of decoration consisting of marquetry made from brass and tortoiseshell. Dining tables were still sometimes rectangular, resting on pillars with claw feet and brass castors; others were round and rested on a heavy central pillar. Similar round tables, some with drawers around the tops, were also used in libraries. Perhaps the best known Regency piece is the circular mirror: convex, in a gilt plaster frame, decorated with gilt balls, and on top an eagle carved on wood or plaster, the latter a motif imported around 1800 from France, where it may have symbolised the glory of Napoleon and his regime. Late Regency style tended towards more naturalistic patterns, in the form of the gilt vine and water-leaf ornament, for example.

Late in the period, a form of severe Greek Classicism re-emerged, thanks partly to the work and writings of Thomas Hope (?1770–1831), the author of *Household Furniture and Decoration* (1807), a book of designs based on his own travels, researches and connoisseurship. Typical of such pieces was the lion monopodium (single-support) stand. Hope also introduced various Indian and Egyptian motifs such as the lotus leaf and hieroglyphics. Sheraton's works *Cabinet Dictionary* (1803) and *Encyclopaedia* (unfinished; 1804–06) reinforced the quest for styles sourced from authentic antiquity.

A large number of Regency items displaying Egyptian influence have a curious characteristic: a head at the top of the piece, and the feet of the same person at the bottom, the two separated by a tapering pilaster that neither bears nor attempts to bear any resemblance to a human body. The Egyptian vogue was strongest between 1804 and 1810, probably as an offshoot of Napoleon's Egyptian campaign. Egyptian temple style was sometimes seen in upward-tapering bookcases. A type of small round table was also popular, that stood on a central pillar resembling a palm tree, with winged cats at its side. On Regency chairs the legs were often in the form of an animal's hind leg.

In the final decade or so of the Georgian period it became clear that inspiration was fading, and taste and quality declining. Simple the designs of that time may have been, but they were also ugly, clumsy and unimaginative. George Smith was notably the author of *A Collection of Designs for Household Furniture and Decoration* (1808), and the more leaden and dull-spirited *The Cabinet Maker and Upholsterer's Guide* (1826); he was also the interpreter and promoter of Hope's ideas and the provider of many useful designs. He particularly referred to the rapid changes in taste that had recently taken place, and blamed the impoverishment of design on 'the necessity for economy urged by so many at the present day'.

A late import that redeemed British interiors was the Biedermeier style, itself a synthesis of English Sheraton, Louis XVI Classicism and the French Empire style. It was characterised by symmetry, predominantly simple geometric shapes and flat surfaces, and the use of columns, mouldings and pediments. Craftsmanship, beautiful materials, comfort and unpretentious practicality were its prime concerns.

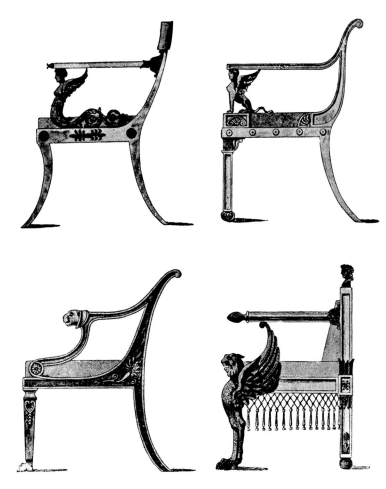

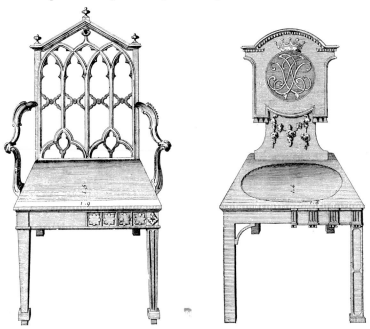

OPPOSITE PAGE: *Examples of chinoiserie designs by J. Mayhew, Chippendale and William Chambers. Furniture in this style typically displayed a sharply angular lattice or trellis pattern. Little carved bells and angular peaks suggestive of pagodas were nearly always to be found, too. Chinese designs appeared on chairs, couches, tables and cabinets, as indeed they did on balustrades and other fixtures.*

ABOVE: *Empire-style designs from George Smith's pattern book,* A Collection of Designs for Household Furniture and Decoration, *1808.*

LEFT: *Gothick designs from Chippendale. The Gothick craze developed from about the 1760s, and in furniture its presence is often recognisable by a pointed-arch device.*

THIS PAGE: *Bedrooms and dressing rooms were often used for receiving visitors, and it was not unusual for the gentleman or lady of the house to entertain friends while actually in bed or while dressing.*

Bedrooms

The placement of bedrooms in a Georgian house varied tremendously according to the date of building and the prevailing customs, the location of the house – Britain or the colonies, town or country – and the style and size of the house.

In the early Georgian period, anterooms, cabinets, bedrooms, boudoirs and dressing rooms formed separate sets of apartments in the great houses for husband, wife and guests. The bedrooms and dressing rooms were treated like any other state room insofar as they were used for receiving visitors: it was not uncommon for the gentleman or lady of the house to give interviews or hold conversations with friends while actually in bed or while dressing. The segregation of the sexes began to disappear around the middle of the eighteenth century and house plans reflected this freer mixing with en suite rooms with wide folding doors. In a typical English villa of that time the principal floor contained only four rooms – hall, saloon, dining room and library. The bedrooms were almost always above the main floor. Many of the great Georgian houses of America of more than one storey had a central area containing one or several of the following: drawing room, ballroom, dining room, music room, study, library, reception room, kitchen, service areas and one or more bedrooms. The house built at Mount Vernon, Fairfax County, Virginia, for George Washington contained, on the ground floor, a state banquet room, music room and west parlour to one side of the entrance hall, and a sitting room, dining room, pantry and library to the other. Arcades on either side led to the state kitchen and office, and to the family kitchen and scullery respectively. The bedroom for Washington and his wife lay on the first floor. Arcades, galleries, covered corridors or halls were indeed commonly found on the ground floor connecting the central area of the house with side wings, and it was in these wings that the bedrooms were sometimes placed (as, for example, at Whitehall, near Annapolis, Maryland, built from 1765–70). On the other hand, Doughoregan Manor, in Howard County, Maryland, lived in by Charles Carroll of Carrollton, one of the signatories of the Declaration of Independence, boasted eleven bedrooms, all located on the upper floor and several of them accessible only via at least one other. The trend, however, noticeable earlier in English houses, was away from these long interconnecting strings of rooms and towards a more compact groundplan with corridors and passages.

In town houses, the larger of which normally had three or four storeys, the principal bedrooms would be on the first floor, customarily at the front of the house. Other, less important bedrooms, assigned to the children or the lodger, would be on the wholly less desirable second floor, while the servants, if they were lucky enough not to be accommodated in the basement,

LEFT: *Traditional 'tester' beds, with four posts, or a solid headboard at the top end and two posts at the bottom, were common throughout the Georgian period.*

BELOW: *A Gothick-style bed designed by Thomas Chippendale. The pointed arch was a distinguishing motif of the Gothick style.*

BOTTOM: *Chaises longues designed by Thomas Sheraton. Items of furniture such as these might be found in the sitting room which often accompanied the main bedroom in grander houses.*

THIS PAGE: *A selection of designs for bedroom furniture to be found in pattern books. The designers of the period, notably Chippendale, Sheraton and Hepplewhite, included even the humble washstand in their style guides.*

OPPOSITE PAGE: *A bed in the grand manner, designed by Chippendale, 1759. Like many of the time, this bed had a headboard and two posts.*

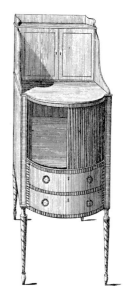

had lodgings in the attic, the plainest part of the house, the beds in some cases having to be let down from the attic walls. As throughout the house, so too the bedrooms descended in terms of quality of decorations, fittings and appointments the further they ascended the house. Decorative schemes were generally lighter and more informal in bedrooms than in reception rooms. Manuals of the early nineteenth century recommended blues and yellows as suitable colours to set off the bed linen that by then was predominantly white. Servants' chambers were of course decked out in any colours or materials that did least damage to the owners' pocket: cheap paints or inexpensive wallpapers, few or no skirting mouldings, simple box cornices and plain doors. In fact, little attention was paid to designing furniture especially for bedrooms, even for the principal ones. The main reception rooms enjoyed the latest fashions and the best pieces made from

the finest materials. When a piece became outdated it was shunted upstairs to one of the bedrooms. Even in the greater houses, furniture made from walnut was found perfectly acceptable in bedrooms, long after mahogany had chased it out of reception rooms.

Towards the end of the seventeenth century, in some households – except the most exalted, where formality still prevailed – the master and mistress might be fortunate enough to have a private sanctum, a small room called a closet. Seclusion was one thing, and quite distinct from the overwhelming domestic taboos that descended in the Victorian period, when etiquette required the strictest segregation between the sexes and between different members of the household, a custom that would not be satisfied except by the creation of physically separate areas and access to them. A liking for privacy coincided with increasingly generous provision of small separate tables in which cosmetics and toiletries could be kept. Along with these went swing mirrors on simple stands which, like the tables, also held drawers. The plates of mirror glass were smallish and thin and accordingly two were used, one large and another about half its size. On a mirror of this sort the join is clearly visible about two-thirds of the way up the frame. The practice continued until the later eighteenth century when new technologies permitted the making of larger sheets of glass.

Traditional 'tester' beds, with four posts, or a solid headboard at the top end and two posts at the bottom, were still common. The elaborate headboard might be carved from pinewood and covered with material, and the whole would be richly upholstered and hung with voluminous drapery. Mattresses were expensive, then as now, especially if filled with goose feathers. The chest of drawers had appeared around 1650, and by the 1720s had developed into a type sometimes called a 'bachelor's chest', probably because clothes could be laid out for brushing on its folding top. This folding top was later replaced by a thin, baize-topped shelf that slid out from the body of the piece.

Another common item by now was the two-stage tallboy, constructed in two separate parts, standing on bracket feet and topped by an overhanging cornice or a pediment. This piece was of Dutch origin and originally known as a 'chest-upon-chest'. Small dressing tables resembling little desks were also made, some having cabriole legs and all having solid, shaped back plates.

Around 1750 mahogany furniture at last began to be seen more frequently in the bedroom. The elaborately carved head and pillars of beds, now no longer swathed in draperies, became the focus of attention. Commodes – meaning cupboards or two- or three-drawer chests, not containers for concealing chamber pots, a nineteenth-century designation – were also frequently to be found in bedrooms, often decorated with metal mounts. Settees were also to be found in boudoirs. Thomas Chippendale in his *Director* offered ideas for chests and clothes cupboards as well as some of the earliest designs for pieces specifically intended for use by gentlemen in bedrooms and dressing rooms, including basin stands and shaving tables, both with basins, swing mirrors and drawers. Chippendale's designs for ladies' dressing tables were creations of huge extravagance.

Chinoiserie design was at this time applied to bedrooms as well as to their furniture and fittings. Famous examples of chinoiserie in America are the bedrooms of Whitehall, near Annapolis, Maryland, and Gunston Hall, built (from 1755) by William Buckland (1734–74), an English émigré craftsman, where the front parlour has rows of shark's teeth projecting from the window and door heads and diagonal ornamentation on the window frames. In England, Saltram House, Devon, has several rooms entirely conceived in the Chinese style; in one bedroom

of Parliament 1759. *J. Taylor Sculp.*

Chinese pictures on glass with Rococo gilt frames match the wallpaper. Demand for breakfast tables arose out of a growing custom of taking breakfast privately in one's own bedroom.

The domination of the mid-Georgian period by the Adam style naturally manifested itself in bedrooms and dressing rooms, as throughout the house. A famous example is the Etruscan Dressing Room at Osterley Park House, Hounslow, Middlesex (remodelled by Robert Adam c.1761–81), which opens out from and is designed to complement the bedroom. In general, however, Adam ignored all bedroom furniture – he is known to have designed three beds only, although the one he designed for Osterley was a wonderfully ornate creation with a dome and extravagant roof hangings. It was left to Hepplewhite to produce designs for down-to-earth items such as chests of

RIGHT: *A French design for a grand bedroom with built-in wardrobes and a bed which is set into an alcove.*

BELOW AND BOTTOM RIGHT: *Designs for bed pillars and Rococo cornices for bed heads or windows by Chippendale.*

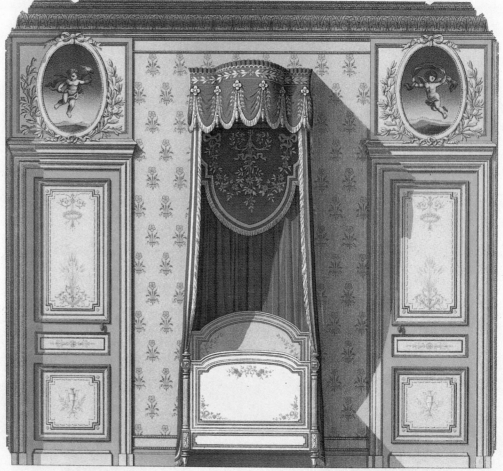

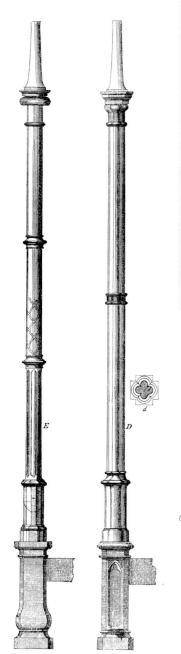

OPPOSITE PAGE: *Beds such as this carved oak example from the early Georgian period gave way to four-posters with elaborate headboards which might be carved from pinewood and covered with material. The whole would be richly upholstered and hung with voluminous drapery.*
BYLAW THE FURNITURE MAKERS

drawers, essentially the same as those in twentieth-century use, and washstands. Sheraton, too, followed with designs for what he called 'corner bason stands', some of which comprised cisterns for storing water. From the 1760s to the 1780s it was fashionable to adopt a scheme of decorating the walls of dressing rooms with engravings set in printed borders imitating frames and hung about with festoons and other decorative motifs in the same material. A distinctive and curious item from the

Regency period was the tent or field bed, with draperies hung from a post or posts and arranged over the headboard and footboard to resemble a tent. In the most sophisticated models, the posts supported a dome. Similar draperies adorned a sofa bedstead, which stood against the wall; the draperies hung from the sofa itself or from a semi-dome canopy affixed to the wall.

On the whole, however, bedroom furniture remained simpler and more purely functional.

Kitchens and Sanitation

If you live in a Georgian house, the chances are that the kitchen has changed beyond all recognition since its original owners were there. Kitchens have long been the hub of a household and nowadays are used, except on rather formal occasions, for entertaining. As much as any other room, the kitchen is now an expression of the owners' identity and lifestyle.

By contrast, in Georgian times, in better homes at least, the kitchen was kept at both a physical and a social distance from the rest of the house, appreciated only by the servants whose domain it almost exclusively was. Relegated in the typical terraced house to the ground floor or the basement, to a separate structure across a large rear yard if the house had one, or, in the great houses of Britain and America, to an adjoining wing or subsidiary building, the kitchen was purely functional. It had no pretensions to beauty or elegance, but it worked, surprisingly well, in fact. One notable difference between the late twentieth-century kitchen and its counterpart of two centuries earlier is the modern obsession with built-in furniture. In Georgian times, very little was fixed; moreover, such storage spaces as existed, such as shelves and dressers, were almost invariably left open.

The Georgian kitchen was designed around a large central working table, which was sturdy and plain and, like floors and shelves, easy to keep clean by scrubbing. Ceilings and walls were usually limewashed.

In the oldest British houses, cooking was done on the floor of an open hearth. The fire in it was kept going constantly between the end of summer and the middle of the following spring. By 1700 this practice had given way to the use of the grate, which was a wrought-iron basket on legs, used over a raised hearth with a huge chimney. By about 1750 the 'perpetual oven', combining oven and grate, had become available, and by the 1780s the enclosed cast-iron cooking range, consisting of iron boiler, grate and oven, had evolved for use with either wood or coal. The grate patented in 1783 by Joseph Langmead became the standard type until well into the twentieth century, although naturally in some humbler dwellings open fires were used contemporaneously for cooking, whether from necessity or choice.

Georgian ingenuity produced some useful gadgetry, such as spits turned by a clockwork device, by a weight-driven 'spit engine' or by a 'smokejack', which harnessed the updraught up the chimney. There were also iron swinging cranes, for supporting pans and kettles – these were adjustable in height; iron racks, dripping pans, pan supports called trivets that were attached to the grate and swung out over the fire; and of course

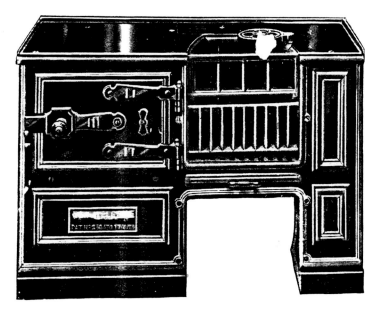

cooking containers such as kettles, pots and skillets. Kitchenware might be made of brass, iron, pewter, copper or tin.

It was during this era that sinks and indoor plumbing began to appear. Mains water, not universally available in the early eighteenth century, was supplied, usually to the kitchen only, in wooden pipes. Sculleries, used for dishwashing, wet-food preparation and all 'dirty housework', and previously little more than roofed-over spaces that protected access to the water pump, became incorporated into the house, complete with a large sink surrounded by plenty of scrubbable working surfaces and a plate-draining rack. The scullery area was often placed behind a partition to separate it from the rest of the kitchen. Early Georgian sinks were usually made of stone – sometimes hewn from a single piece – or wood and lined with lead, until by 1800 ceramic sinks were becoming readily available. Soapstone, referred to as 'tin', was also used.

A walk-in larder for storing food was a common feature of Georgian kitchens and there might also be a pantry, in which provisions and table furnishings were kept or cleaned. The main items of furniture were still the central table, often made of ash, and one or more dressers, joined later by tall cupboards for dried goods, preserves and spare china and kitchenware. These items were generally made of softwood and styled so as to match the

wall panelling that gradually replaced plastered walls. Since kitchens were often below ground-level they could be rather dark; to add some light, the application of a white limewash to the ceiling was common. Furniture styling depended a great deal on the location and role of the kitchen in the house, but plain finishes and painted, easily cleanable surfaces remained the norm. Actual working surfaces were left unpainted and were cleaned by scrubbing or sanding. Floors and shelves, too, were scrubbable.

Most important houses in the eighteenth century had a sunken ice-house at a cool, well-drained spot somewhere in the garden. Winter ice could be stored in it for up to two years, and the ice could be used for making ice cream, keeping wine cool and certain therapeutic purposes such as treating sprains. Food was also stored in the ice-house. Ice-houses were usually egg- or igloo-shaped structures of brick or stone and entered down steps with or without an intervening passage and one or more doors.

THIS PAGE AND OPPOSITE: A selection of cooking stoves and utensils which might have been found in a Georgian kitchen. By the 1780s the enclosed cast-iron cooking range consisting of iron boiler, grate and oven had become the standard type, and it continued in use until well into the twentieth century.

TOP LEFT AND CENTRE LEFT: *The dresser as we now think of it evolved during the eighteenth century from the court cupboards of the sixteenth century.*
BYLAW THE FURNITURE MAKERS

LEFT: *A Georgian-style kitchen. The fittings may not be authentic, but the large central table was certainly regarded as an essential aid to food preparation at that time.*

ABOVE: *A hand-painted Georgian-inspired kitchen, with a theme of eighteenth-century-style pilasters, cornices, mouldings and raised and fielded panels.*

LEFT: *In the Georgian kitchen very little was fixed; moreover, such storage spaces as existed, such as shelves and dressers, were almost invariably left open. Whilst this would not be appropriate for the twentieth-century kitchen, modern manufacturers try to incorporate design elements to recreate the 'feel' of the period without the inconvenience.*

BELOW AND BOTTOM: *Kitchens of the period, such as these in Williamsberg, Virginia, USA, were purely functional with no pretensions to either beauty or elegance. The main items of furniture were the central table and one or more dressers for the storing of dry goods. The actual work surfaces were left unpainted and were cleaned by scrubbing.*

Bathing and Sanitation

Bathing was not an important preoccupation of the Georgians; however, once Beau Brummel made the connection between cleanliness and elegance, the demand for water grew to flood proportions. Technology brought improvements to sanitation: steam engines for pumping water (1810), cast-iron mains (1827), filtration (1829) and reservoirs. Meanwhile, however, cleanliness could be attended to, from time to time, as the mood took one, by visiting one of the public baths that existed in London and some other cities. A few rudimentary showers could be bought by 1820, though only the most daring of householders owned one. During the second half of the eighteenth century some middle-class homes incorporated simple plunge baths that would be filled by water brought from the kitchen, where it was heated in the boiler. The bath itself would be placed in a bedroom. Most householders in late Georgian homes in England and America could not afford to pay for water to be pumped to the upper floors (a 'high service') and made do instead with a

mains supply to the ground floor only (the 'low service'). A variant of the hot bath was the cold-water plunge bath, sometimes a stone-lined creation sited in the lower levels of the house or, more rarely, a marble bath in a marble-walled bathroom often situated in the garden.

From about the 1820s, bathrooms were slowly introduced into the houses of the upper classes. From then on, the water would be heated under the bath itself. In poorer houses, where there was no bathroom and no piped water, people took a bath in a portable, flat-bottomed and roll-topped tin tub, which might be set up in a kitchen and filled and emptied by hand.

Wrought-iron tripod washstands with pewter basins appeared in the 1750s, to be followed in the 1770s by elegant, quarter-circle mahogany or rosewood washstands with raised, shaped backs, round bowls and indentations to take the soap. All these pieces for toiletry, including shaving tables and bidets – introduced from France – were used in dressing rooms in the better houses and discreetly disguised under and behind tops,

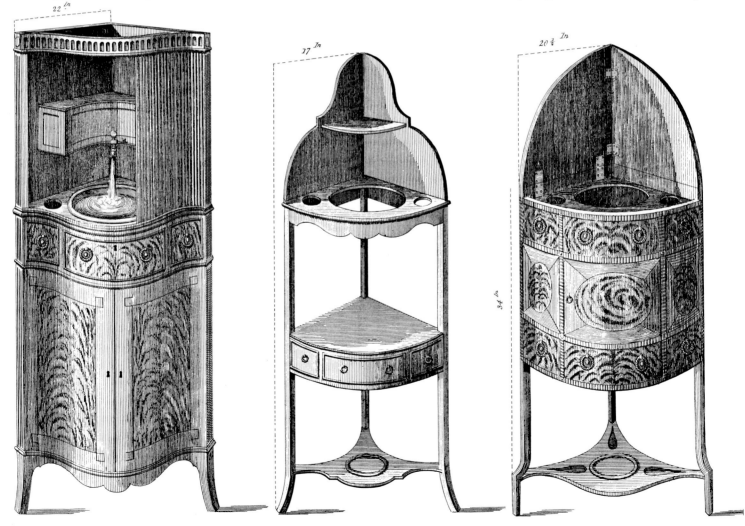

shelves and other cabinetwork. The bedroom chamber pot was also concealed in a superior bedside table or a cabinet.

A water closet patented in 1775 by Alexander Cumming of London (a watchmaker, straying off the track of his usual business!) incorporated an S-bend pipe that provided a seal of water below the pan and so prevented gases or smells from filtering back up from the drain. Soon afterwards, in 1778, Joseph Bramah (a cabinetmaker) patented another type of valve closet, with a flap trap at the bottom operated by pulling up a handle at the side. William Kent provided for a water closet off the entrance hall at Holkham Hall, Norfolk; Robert Adam for four at Luton Hoo, Bedfordshire, and the actor David Garrick had an extravagant three in his town house at the Adelphi along London's Thames Embankment, although he modestly installed only a single one at his country house at Hampton, Middlesex. By 1822 the best houses did have at least one water closet, and some even had one for the servants. Most Georgian houses, however, lacked any such amenity.

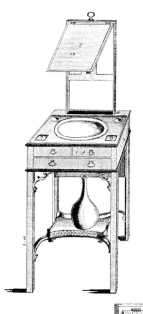

THIS PAGE AND OPPOSITE: *A selection of Sheraton's designs for toiletry equipment. Pieces such as these, including shaving tables and bidets – introduced from France – were used in dressing rooms in the better houses and discreetly disguised under and behind tops, shelves and other cabinetwork. The bedroom chamber pot was also concealed in a superior bedside table or cabinet.*

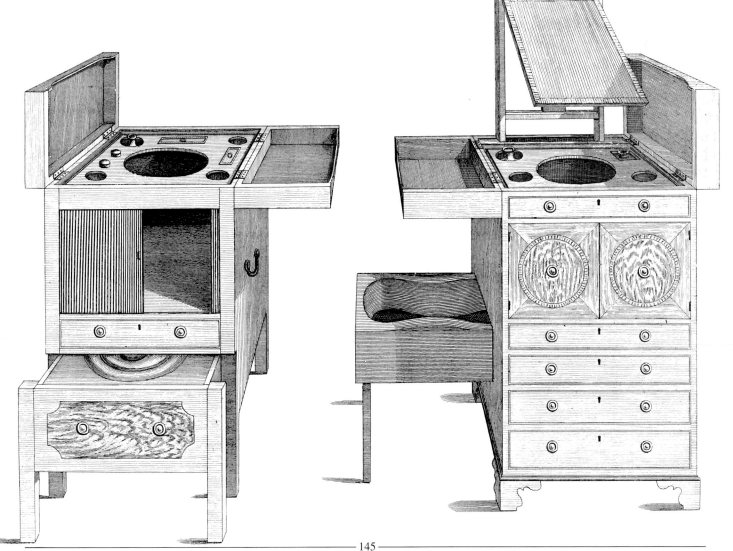

Chapter 4
Interior Details

'Commenced taking off Roof of the House to be replaced by a new one, to get rid of the evils of flat roofing and spouts and gutters – or in other words, to supersede the Jeffersonian by the Common Sense Plan.'

General John Hartwell Cocke, diary, 19 September 1836, of his house Bremo, in Fluvanna County, Virginia, USA, built in 1819 by Thomas Jefferson

Until the late seventeenth century, doors usually consisted of vertical planks bound with horizontal ledges or ties at the back, fixed in place by wooden pegs or soft wrought-iron nails. However, by 1700 the six-panelled door, which was to remain the pre-eminent type during the whole Georgian period in Britain and the contemporary Classical period in America, had become standard as the front door, and often in interiors too, for all homes of any importance. Interior doors sometimes had six, sometimes only four or two panels. Oak and mahogany doors were much favoured and often replaced earlier plank doors, especially internally. Panelled doors were found throughout the social scale. In less wealthy houses, excellent craftsmanship often compensated for the use of cheaper woods. In the smallest eighteenth-century town houses, where six panels would be out of place against the proportions of the elevation, four panels were more usual.

The typical early Georgian arrangement strictly reproduced Palladian principles. The panels were disposed in the same proportions as the windows in a façade: the largest occupied the centre, slightly smaller panels were at the bottom, while the top panels were by far the smallest. Variations were many. Pairs of panels might be fused together, making a door of seven, five or three panels. The two lowest panels of external doors most often received this treatment; joined together, the panels would be raised flush with the frame. This gave a hardier surface better able to withstand kicks and knocks.

By the end of the eighteenth century, doors with two or three sunken panels had become more common. The rules of eighteenth-century proportion required doors to be a little more than twice as high as they were wide. In the Regency period the classic door had two tall, round-headed panels running between the top and bottom rails. By the early nineteenth century multiple bead mouldings, called reeded surrounds, were often used to mark the edges of the panels in internal doors, and corners were emphasised by paterae – round, flat ornaments in low relief, each inset with a circular panel or other decorative motif. Door mouldings became lighter and more subtle during the course of the eighteenth century, and door furniture more delicate but also more elaborate. Broken pediments (open at the top) were frequently used from the mid-eighteenth century onwards, especially above interior doors.

Georgian doors were nearly always painted; if not, they were polished with many layers of wax. Wood was rarely left unadorned. Woodworm readily attacks bare wood but makes no impression on paint. Besides, the Georgians took pains to conceal inferior wood and would have been shocked by the late twentieth-century fashion for stripped wood. Front doors were usually painted a dark colour, such as dark green or brown, or perhaps 'grained' in imitation of seasoned oak or other exotic woods. The surrounds were painted broken white or 'stone'. Similar dark shades, such as chocolate brown, matched by dark skirting, were popular indoors. The paints used in the eighteenth century were thinner than those used now, and contained lead. Often the brushstrokes remained visible, an effect which can be reproduced by dragging a coat of tinted scumble glaze (opaque or semi-opaque colour) over a surface coat of oil-based paint.

THIS PAGE AND OPPOSITE: *A range of designs for interior doors and doorcases from American pattern books, including those of Asher Benjamin. The door illustrated above demonstrates typical Palladian proportions.*

THIS PAGE: *A selection of interior doors with both functional and charmingly decorative door furniture.*

Windows and Window Treatments

By 1700 all sash windows in Britain were fitted with interior shutters made strongly of wooden boards, sometimes hinged and folding, concertina-fashion, sometimes sliding horizontally or vertically. Shutters and their hinges were constructed in essentially the same way as doors, and developed in a similar way; they were often operated by small brass rings. Wooden or wrought-iron bars, and brass or iron hooks were used to secure them. Horizontally opening shutters were often housed in a reveal of the inside wall. Later, when shortage of space became an issue, shutters were stored not in shutter-boxes at each side of the window, but in cavities built into the sills below, from which they had to be pulled up by brass handles fixed to the tops. Shutters themselves were often embellished with panels on the section that was visible when they were in the reveal. Internal shutters of the Georgian period were often horizontally divided into two or three separately hinged sections. Opening the top section only allowed some daylight in, while protecting furniture and fittings from damaging direct light. Fixed shutters were in some houses supplemented by small, removable shutters or screens that covered the lower portion of the window only and afforded additional privacy. These so-called 'snob screens' were always painted green. For further security, some shutters were equipped with an alarm in the form of bells. Removable iron bars called pullbars, slotted into holes on either side of the shutters, served as an additional deterrents to intruders.

Exterior shutters, usually painted green or some other dark colour, were commonplace in the Georgian period, though few survive in Britain. On the eastern seaboard of America, however, external shutters are still to be found; they were fitted in the early days as protection from the weather, a function that was later assumed by storm windows, leaving shutters as decorative features only. External roller blinds were also very popular in the late Georgian period in Britain, and in the Federal period in America. These were usually made of sturdy canvas, often brightly striped, and were drawn up into painted wooden boxes, a few of which survive – nearly always minus the blinds themselves. With the introduction of pine window frames in the eighteenth century, it became normal to paint the wood, most often with white lead paint or another light colour. Georgian 'white' paint was in fact usually 'broken' – mixed with tiny amounts of darker paints to add to the richness of the effect. This paint was often referred to as 'stone' colour. Later in the century, however, dark colours enjoyed some popularity: dark grey, brown (with imitation oak graining) and green (especially on Regency window joinery) were favoured, although often these shades have been overpainted in cream, white or even, in the twentieth century, an inappropriate pillar-box red.

LEFT AND BELOW LEFT: *Internal shutters of the Georgian period were often horizontally divided into two or three separately hinged sections. Opening the top section only allowed some daylight in, while protecting furniture and fittings from damaging direct light.*

BELOW: *Full-length, arch-topped windows admit maximum light to a living room.*
HADDONSTONE

Roller blinds were widely available by 1700. In early versions, the canvas or cloth was attached to a tin case housing a spring, and was often dyed or painted green; later in the century it became fashionable to match the main curtains. Venetian blinds were also in widespread use in the Georgian period. The name is thought to derive not from an origin in Venice, but from their use in covering Venetian or Palladian windows, which were popular throughout the first half of the eighteenth century. Neither form of blind was known for its reliability: the fabric and, in the case of Venetian blinds, the laths, too, often became detached from the roller or the tape.

Curtains and Furnishing Fabrics

'Sub-curtains' were sometimes hung in late Georgian houses to protect furnishings and decorations from direct daylight. They were made of a plain white cambric then known as 'muslin', or of cotton finely spun in a variety of thicknesses and textures. These fabrics were imported into Britain and the colonies from India until 1779, when the invention of the spinning mule made their production in Britain itself possible. Full window curtains replaced simple cloth hangings in the early Georgian period in finer houses only, but by the 1730s they were a feature of every domestic interior. They were drawn horizontally, along a rod, or vertically, using cords, and they could be in one or two pieces. By 1765, as Benjamin Franklin wrote, the fashion was 'to make one Curtain only for each window'. The festoon, easily the most popular type in Britain and America, was made of light fabric and thus could be drawn up vertically in swags. The lines that pulled the curtains ran through two vertical lines of brass rings on the back of the material, up over the boxwood pulleys behind a pelmet or board, and down to a fastening near the dado rail. A variant of the festoon was the two-part drapery curtain, consisting of two pieces of material drawn up towards the outer corners of the window, where they formed heavy swags.

By 1780 festoons and drapery curtains were fast fading from popularity. Instead, house-owners were choosing 'French draw'

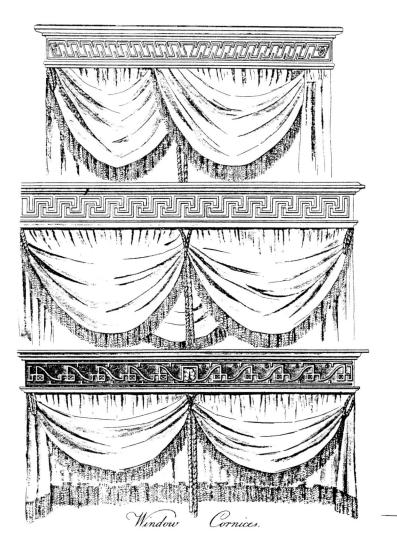

Window Cornices.

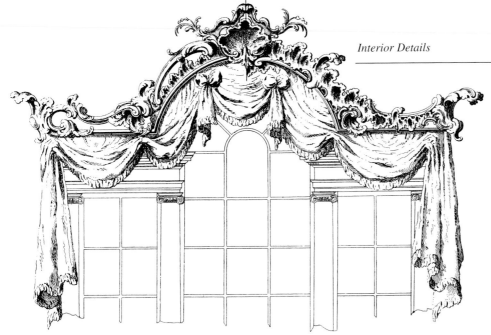

OPPOSITE PAGE: *A selection of designs for window treatments from pattern books of the period. Full window curtains replaced simple cloth hangings in the early Georgian period in finer houses only, but by the 1730s they were a feature of every domestic interior. By 1765, in the words of Benjamin Franklin the fashion was 'to make one Curtain only for each window'.*

THIS PAGE: *Designs for window treatments from Chippendale (top) and Sheraton (below).*

RIGHT: *An attractive modern interpretation of Georgian-style curtains, wallpaper and upholstery fabric.* SANDERSONS

OPPOSITE PAGE, LEFT: *Modern interior fabrics in the Regency style.* SANDERSONS

OPPOSITE PAGE, RIGHT: *Window cornices and drapery for drawing rooms, from London pattern books of 1805–6.*

or 'French rod' draperies, in which a pair of curtains was drawn horizontally, the two pieces of material being hung by wooden or brass rings to a rod above the window. These were the forerunners of the horizontally drawn curtains of the twentieth century. In the Regency period, rooms, including even the ceiling, could be swathed almost entirely in curtaining, producing an effect known as the 'tent-room'. Somewhat less ostentatiously, curtains might be massed into a display called 'continuous drapery', in which material would sweep in bulky swags from one side of a pelmet to another. Such extravagance

was normally only lavished on the most opulent and largest of the rooms. Small, modest rooms would have had correspondingly plain, understated curtains.

During the Georgian period, curtain materials became increasingly lightweight. Until about the 1770s, a favourite fabric was 'tabby', a silk of alternate satin and watered stripes, often dyed gold. Moreens were also popular, lined with light cotton or with a worsted material called tammy. Industrial advances in Britain facilitated the production of furnishing fabrics such as lighter cotton and linens sporting printed

patterns, and of the previously highly expensive silks. An important feature of these fabrics was washability. In 1722 a ban was placed on the importation from India, and their use for clothing and furnishings, of printed and dyed cottons, in order to protect native British industry which relied heavily on export to the American colonies. In 1774, British cotton calicoes were released from this restriction on use, although the ban on imports from India remained in force.

British cloth – made with three blue lines running through the warp to distinguish it from imports – became immediately popular for use in interior furnishings. Chintzes (cottons glazed for resilience and lustre) with bold flower patterns were especially popular, as were brightly coloured calicoes. Such fabrics could tolerate repeated washings without fading. In 1759 George Washington ordered from London some blue chintz-covered furnishings to match his wallpaper. All his American contemporaries relied entirely on Britain for sophisticated

textiles and indeed for all furnishings, at least until after the War of Independence in 1783. Americans certainly attempted to set up a textile industry, some in the face of great challenge and adversity, not to mention the destruction of their factories and materials by the British.

Block-printed cottons, made using pearwood or sycamore blocks, were common in Britain and America in the mid-eighteenth century. By 1770, these were followed by copper plates, of which early versions could print in one colour only, but later versions (late 1780s) in two or three colours. Favourite colours were black, red, blue and purple; yellow made an occasional appearance. Like wallpapers, which were also block-printed, textiles often featured landscapes or other scenes from nature. Copper rollers, introduced in 1783, enabled still more elaborate patterns and colours to be printed. By 1785 colour coordination between cottons, linens, silks and other elements of interior decoration was established as a principle of design.

Walls

Plastering began in Britain as a means of conserving heat, reducing fire risk and strengthening wattle-and-daub walls. Moulded plaster in Britain at that time was called stucco and it was used both internally and externally. In the eighteenth century plastered walls were preferred to panelling in the grand houses, where it was much suited to Palladian and neo-Classical styles. Palladian architects introduced hand-modelled plasterwork and plaster wall panels derived from French patterns. Scenes from mythology, for example, might be set within panels of plaster, and ornamented with pediments and swags. Some houses in Bath dating from 1727 onwards have this feature. In the later eighteenth century the Adam brothers made liberal use of plaster ornament for interior walls.

Some plasters, used for the final coat, were based on burnt gypsum (calcium sulphate) instead of lime, and mixed with animal hair or perhaps straw or reeds for additional binding strength and durability. These plasters, noted for their fast setting time, were applied in three or more coats to a network of laths made of deal, fir, beech or oak. From the turn of the nineteenth century, wire netting stapled or tacked to the joists added robustness to the plaster. The exact composition of the plaster used by the Adam brothers in the mid- to late-eighteenth century is not known, though it too contained gypsum or fibre. Instead of being modelled on the walls it was cast in moulds when hot. The Adams painted the plaster ground in light shades of pink, green or blue to pick out the ornament, although the ornament itself was sometimes also painted. Such individual treatment could not, however, be afforded by most house-owners, so in most homes pre-moulded ornament made in workshops was applied to the top coat of base plaster. Another method of creating ornamentation was to use a press-mould for pressing patterns into wet plaster. A specially shaped tool called – and resembling – a horse was used to apply cornices, dado rails and circular mouldings. By the nineteenth century, plaster mouldings were being mass-produced.

THIS PAGE: *A range of typical plaster mouldings. Palladian architects introduced hand-modelled plasterwork and plaster wall panels derived from French patterns. However, most house-owners could not afford such individual treatment and so pre-moulded ornament was applied to the finished plaster wall.*

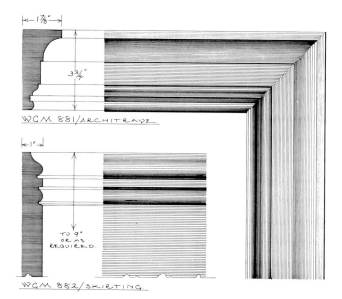

WGM 881/ARCHITRAVE.

WGM 882/SKIRTING.

WGM 91/CORNER A.

WGM 91/CORNER B.

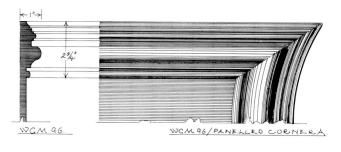

WGM 96.

WGM 96/PANELLED CORNER A.

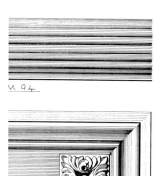

M 94

M 95

95/CORNER A.

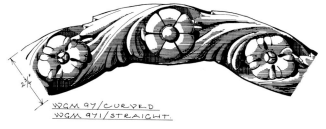

WGM 97/CURVED
WGM 971/STRAIGHT.

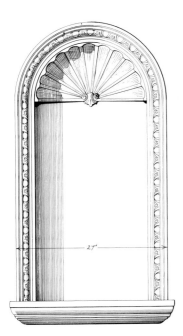

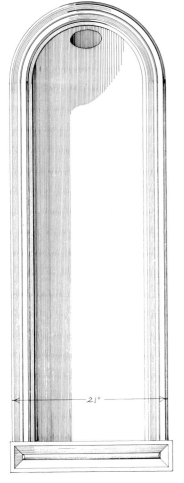

Mouldings first took the form of wooden fittings, used to decorate, or more often to conceal, structural features such as joints or transitions between planes. In Classical interiors, they were often placed to reflect the vertical gradation of a Greek column – the skirting board ('baseboard' in America), dado and cornice of the moulding corresponding to the base, pedestal and entablature respectively of the column. Early mouldings, such as the box cornice and 'bolection' (projection) moulding, which projected beyond the surface of the framing, were pronounced and substantial. During the course of the eighteenth century,

ABOVE: *Examples of Rococo plaster ornament.*

ABOVE LEFT AND LEFT: *From the early eighteenth century, alcoves on either side of the fireplace were turned into niches with plasterwork tops in imitation of styles in the larger houses.*

more mouldings were used for the purposes of concealment and they consequently became flatter and lighter. Although some continued to be made from wood, plaster came· to be increasingly preferred. Skirting boards, on the other hand, were more often of wood, the better to protect plaster walls. In Palladian houses of the 1720s–1760s, moulding was characteristically made in 'egg-and-tongue' (or 'egg-and-dart') motifs, and painted. Neo-Classical mouldings followed by the 1770s, and then, at the end of the century, 'Grecian' decorative motifs. Typically, Regency mouldings consisted simply of beading (in variants known as 'reeding' and 'quirking', an acute, V-shaped groove between a flat piece and a convex moulding) and were used on chimneypieces, cornices, door surrounds, dados and skirtings, often decorated with paterae. The outlines of moulds for dado or chair rails (protecting the area of the wall from scraping chairs) were often the inverse of the skirting board: thus, where one had the greatest projection at the top, the other might have it at the bottom. Dados and other plasterwork could be quite elaborate, with motifs even picked out in gilt,

although most plaster mouldings were painted white or, more often, the same colour as the flat ground. In general, moulded plasterwork was more plentiful and more decorative in the rooms that were likely to be on show; thus modest rooms had only rudimentary mouldings.

Two other plaster derivatives deserve mention. Scagliola, made from pigmented plaster and marble chips and cast and polished to look like marble, was used to create 'marble' columns, floors, chimneypieces and many other elements of an interior. A variant was Marezzo marble, which was made purely from plaster. Papier mâché was made essentially from rag paper, to which various processes were applied, after which it was painted or gilded, to be used as mouldings and ornaments, often to excellent aesthetic effect. A French version was made from pulped paper, glue and whiting, and called *carton pierre*. These products were considerably cheaper, easier to make and lighter than traditional plaster or, of course, the stone they sought to imitate.

Applied wooden pilasters and columns, usually of oak or

OPPOSITE PAGE, LEFT: *A magnificent chinoiserie panel of Dutch tiles, manufactured during the second quarter of the eighteenth century and painted in high temperature colours.*

OPPOSITE PAGE, RIGHT: *Wallpapers which reflect the Georgian predilection for oriental design.*

LEFT: *The plush Green Drawing Room at Clandon Park, Surrey, has plasterwork by the Italian stuccoers Artari and Bagutti. The wallpaper dates from 1735. Above the marble fireplace is a panel with a painted classical scene.*

softwood and sometimes intricately carved, were used in grand houses in the eighteenth century to conceal the joints between the stiles (upright members) and the panels set into them. As wooden panelling for walls went out of fashion, the pilaster strips and columns continued to be applied to add interest to the wall surface or to emphasise windows. When panelling was used, the wood was usually painted with a paint that had a slightly glossy finish with a streaked effect. More rarely, woods of a high quality and colour, such as pine, were left unpainted, being instead finished with beeswax polish.

Wood was the material used for built-in furniture such as chests of drawers, dressers, cupboards and bookshelves. From the early eighteenth century on, the alcoves at each side of the chimney breast were made to house panelled cupboards in town houses in England and America. Some walls, as also doors, cornices and ceilings, were painted. For many centuries, the most frequently used paints had been hand-mixed whitewash with pigments added to give ochre, red, blue and green shades, and limewash, based on slaked lime. For wainscots and other interior woodwork, paints with a glossier finish resulting from an admixture of oil, wax or milk (the forerunners of modern emulsion paint) were favoured. Until the early eighteenth

RIGHT AND ABOVE: *Designs for cornices, dados and other plasterwork could be quite elaborate, with motifs even picked out in gilt, although most plaster mouldings were painted white or, more often, the same colour as the flat ground. In general, moulded plasterwork was more plentiful and more decorative in the rooms that were likely to be on show; thus modest rooms had only rudimentary mouldings.*

RIGHT: *Empire-style stencilled border for walls and cornices. In America, stencilling in distemper was extremely popular, particularly for floorboards and walls.*

century the paint colours of choice for walls, from cornice to skirting board, and for doors as well, were wood colours, various shades of brown that resembled walnut, mahogany, oak or cedar. The skirting and sometimes the shutters were painted a dusty red, deep mahogany or even black. Mouldings were picked out in white or, in the most luxurious houses, gilt. The principle was to create a unified whole, the interior walls resembling as much as possible a complete architectural entity such as a Classical column.

By the 1720s, white – specifically, the 'broken white', a slightly off-white shade that was particularly admired – and other light colours – light greens, blues, pinks and violets – were superseding the dark wood colours. The cheapest whitewash (or distemper – water-based paint) was used on plaster walls and ceilings. Internal woodwork, however, was treated with white lead paint, an oil-based paint, to which could be added pigments to make colours other than white. A matt finish could be achieved by adding a little turpentine to the paint; this was widely used by the 1740s in Britain, but not in America, where gloss finishes were preferred until the end of the century. Strong

colours were not, however, abandoned, and the 'stone' colours, greys, the wood colours and 'chocolate' were cheap to make and continued to be employed widely. Less common, being more expensive to make, were sky blue, pea and olive green. Pink, lemon, orange and 'straw' were dearer still. Ultramarine and smalt, both dark blues obtained from, respectively, lapis lazuli and glass, were beyond the reach of most pockets. From the 1720s, however, in Britain and America, dark blue could be obtained from a paint based on a pigment called Prussian blue, derived from animal blood burnt with alum. Greens and reds were especially popular for libraries and dining rooms. Incidentally, some of the paints used at that time were highly toxic, for instance 'King's yellow' and 'patent yellow'. In the second half of the eighteenth century, archaeological correctness led to the widespread adoption of the colours of ancient Rome and Greece, notably terracotta red. Marbling and graining became fashionable again, but the gilding that was reminiscent of Renaissance Italy and thus characteristic of the Palladian house early in the century largely fell into disuse, although occasionally silver decoration was employed instead.

In some houses, walls were painted not with colour washes but with murals, friezes, *trompe l'oeil* designs and figures, the latter being especially popular in the eighteenth century. *Trompe l'oeil* was done using a range of subjects, including vistas, windows, bookshelves and wall niches. Stencilling has been used as a wall decoration since at least the thirteenth century, or earlier. In America, stencilling in distemper was extremely popular, particularly for floorboards and walls; in Britain its use was mostly confined to rural cottages. Elizabethan wallpapers were sometimes patterned with stencilled designs, or were hand-painted, and stencils were also applied to wallpapers in America from the late 1700s until well into the nineteenth century.

By the late seventeenth century, luxury wallpapers were being imported from China, in large pieces decorated with non-repeating designs of landscapes and other scenes from nature, most notably the famous bird-and-flower motif. These wallpapers were popular in Palladian houses. A cheaper option to choose was 'chinoiserie', papers which imitated Chinese models. While the first English paper employed only black and white, the use of distemper colours thickened with glue, followed from the 1850s by oil colours, made a variety of designs possible: imitation plasterwork, damask or leather geometric shapes, marbling, flowers, architectural motifs such as pillars and arches, urns and niches or simple stripes. While many such patterns and textures have survived the centuries with their positive image intact, flock wallpaper has not. This type of paper, made by sticking powdered wool onto glued paper to simulate cut-pile fabrics, was wildly popular in the mid-eighteenth century not only in Britain, America and the other colonies, but also in France to which it was exported. The American colonies had to rely solely on imported English and Chinese papers, which, like many other luxury goods, were subject to tax, until 1765 when John Rugar established a

ABOVE: *Design for a wall panel, with a depiction of a graceful girl in the central medallion, 1777.*

LEFT: *Designs by Thomas Chippendale of 'borders for damask or paper hangings', 1761.*

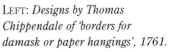

BELOW: *Delft tiles such as shown here were frequently used in fire surrounds. These are of English origin and date from around the middle of the eighteenth century.*

BELOW: *Delft tiles such as shown here were frequently used in fire surrounds. These are of English origin and date from around the middle of the eighteenth century.*

wallpaper factory in New York. After the Revolution, wallpaper and many other household products were made successfully and on a large scale by native manufacturers.

Some of the earliest wallpapers were tacked on to plaster. Later they were usually stretched on canvas over a wooden frame, and a cavity left between wall and canvas, which incidentally has aided their conservation. From the early eighteenth century until about 1800, papers were glued onto a canvas lining, and this was tacked or pasted onto the plaster wall. In the Regency period, a fad developed for applying varnish to papers.

Floors and Floor Coverings

By the early eighteenth century, the upper classes were installing wooden block floors of oak, elm or yew in their houses. For more general use, deal boards were the norm. Tongued and grooved boards were introduced in the 1820s: these were increasingly machine-made, and of a lesser, and more uniform width. The timber was also well seasoned.

Timber became standard for ground floors during the nineteenth century, although not until 1860 did the law require such floors to have an air gap beneath them. Other solid floors continued to be laid, however. These might consist of earth and clay; brick or kiln-built paviors (similar to bricks but less deep); square, non-porous quarry tiles; flagstones or other arrangements of stone. From the seventeenth century the great houses used Portland stone or English marble from Purbeck, Sussex, Kent and Derbyshire. Many British houses had floors of slabs of the local stone.

The smartest houses had been using carpets as floor coverings since the early seventeenth century, even when the floors were made of good quality deal or oak. Alternatives to carpets included stencilled patterns, plain-coloured floors, plaster floors made from the addition of pigments to plaster of Paris, and floorcloths in strong colours and geometric patterns, as well as the traditional simple mats of woven rush, reed, straw or grass. Painted or glazed flooring remained popular even when cheap carpets became available towards the end of the eighteenth century. The floor of a whole room might be coloured, or just the borders round the carpet, and these were usually painted in the same colour as the other woodwork in the room.

Oil cloths were very popular throughout the eighteenth and nineteenth centuries in both Britain and America, on their own or as a surround to a central carpet. The patterns were often floral, with designs that as much as possible resembled Turkish carpets or any other sought-after style. Often they featured *trompe l'oeil* designs that made them resemble stone, marble, mosaic pavement or wood. Sometimes oil-cloths were left plain, as for example the 'canvas floor cloth, painted green', commissioned by Thomas Jefferson for the South Dining

Room at Monticello, the home he designed for himself.

During the second half of the eighteenth century, the Industrial Revolution gave a boost to British carpet manufacturers, which in turn led to a boom in carpet ownership. British machine-made knotted or pile carpets in oriental styles were in place in very many ordinary households by 1840. Carpet workshops appeared in Britain from the mid-1730s, including the most famous at Wilton in Wiltshire, Axminster in Dorset and Kidderminster in Worcestershire. In June 1778 the famous cabinetmaker Thomas Chippendale recommended to his client, Sir Edward Knatchbull, the purchase, through himself, of an Axminster carpet for the drawing-room at Mersham le Hatch, Kent:

...to Correspond with your Ceiling to go into the Bow and at equal distances from the plinth all round the Room, the Expense of it will be according to their best Price about £100 they will have a painting to make of it at large and the Colours to buy on purpose... .

As it happened, Chippendale was so notoriously unbusinesslike that the baronet went elsewhere for his carpet, buying one from Thomas Moore of Moorfields, London, at the substantially lower price of £57 12s.

In these great country houses, the practice was to match carpet to ceiling and other elements of the décor. Moore was also a favourite manufacturer of the architect Robert Adam and was commissioned by him to make carpets for Saltram, Devon. The dining-room carpet reflects the design of the ceiling: a shell-filled circle in the middle, segmental panels against the circumference and scrolls beyond. The saloon carpet mirrored, at least in the centre, the design of the ceiling.

Wilton and Kidderminster carpets were cheaper than the knotted carpets made at Axminster and Moorfields. They were made on looms and were usually made in strips, which could then be cut to accommodate the shape of the floor. Such fitted carpets were fashionable by the mid-eighteenth century.

Among the more functional floor coverings in use in Georgian times were 'ingrain' carpets, made (in Scotland) from two intersecting webs of cloth, to make reversible carpets, or after 1822, from three webs, which produced colourful carpets with a different pattern on each side. Ingrain carpets were used to cover hallways, stairs and servants' rooms. A variant was the flat-woven 'Venetian carpet', made after about 1800 in both Britain and America and recognisable by its striped pattern. Druggets were carpet covers, made of baize, serge or haircloth, which served to keep the dirt off luxury carpets and protect them from wear. In less wealthy homes, druggets were the only floor coverings. Other utilitarian and robust floor coverings were paper carpets, and in American homes especially, 'list' or 'selvedge' carpets, made from fragments of cloth.

THIS PAGE: *Solid floors with inlaid or stencilled designs were frequently employed in the Georgian period. Portland stone, marble, slate and timber were popular materials.*

Ceilings

In the early Georgian period, ceilings of town houses were generally plain, the cornice providing interest, although in the decorative scheme cornices were often treated as part of the wall and painted in the same colour. Cornices of this period were often rather handsome, perhaps featuring the Corinthian order, with its scrolled modillions (ornamental brackets), row of close-set dentils (square blocks) and rich mouldings. A spacious hall might be correspondingly decorated with columns of pilasters of the same order, and the ceiling over the staircase given a simple geometric design. Ceiling plasterwork remained highly decorative in Palladian houses in Britain and America until about the middle of the eighteenth century. Relief plasterwork, representing dolphins, badges and pendants, leaves and Classical features, was much sought after in all grades of Georgian house.

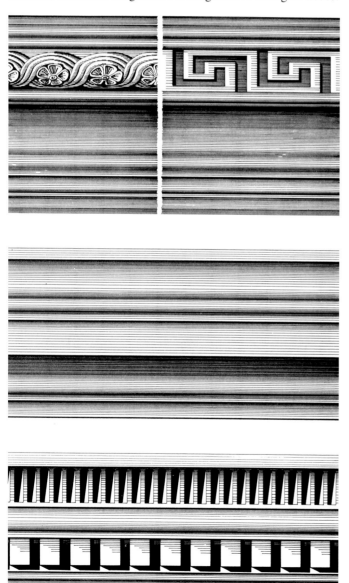

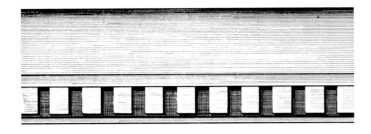

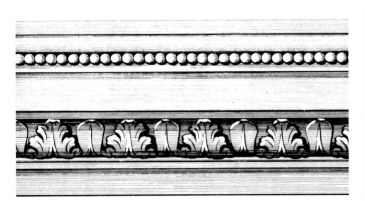

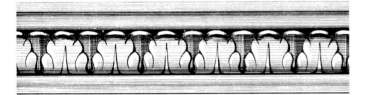

THIS PAGE AND OPPOSITE: *A range of cornices, roses and ornamented ceilings. Plasterwork on ceilings continued to be highly decorative in Palladian houses in Britain and America until* the mid-eighteenth century, and was much sought after in all grades of Georgian house.

OVERLEAF: *Two highly decorated ceilings in the style of Robert Adam (left) and Louis XV (right).*

Houses of the period in Dublin bear witness to a curious historical circumstance – the presence in Ireland of Italian plasterers from France; they created some extravagant schemes portraying skies and heavenly scenes with borders of leaves. This style was picked up by local craftsmen in the 1740s, with the result that grand ceilings are to be found in even fairly modest houses.

From about 1750 to 1790 cornices became lighter and more distant from any of the Classical orders; mouldings, too, became smaller and simpler. Coloured ceilings with white relief were occasionally found. The work of the Adam brothers was characterised by grace and restraint. Ornament was never overdone, and curves or regular geometric shapes were enhanced by soft, light colours – lilacs, pinks and greens, occasionally relieved by Pompeian red or some other deeper hue. In an Adam interior, or a contemporary interior that reflected their influence, the ceiling, exquisitely designed and wrought, was often the *pièce de résistance*. Grecian or Etruscan

ornament was employed for ceilings, friezes and walls; grisaille panels (greyish-tinted imitation low-relief), cameos or medallions were common in the grander houses. In more modest houses, plain plaster walls and ceilings, sometimes treated with an 'Adam' colour wash, and a straightforward cornice were usual. The simplest houses of all, such as farmhouses and cottages, had the long-traditional ceilings of floorboards and joists of plain timber, usually whitewashed or painted.

By Regency times, elaborate friezes and cornices were thought to be overblown and tasteless. While the showier houses were full of profuse and lavish ornament, with stuccoed and painted ceilings, more often decoration in cast or modelled plaster was restrained, being confined to a cornice spreading to the flat of the ceiling. From about 1820, when gas lighting had been introduced and the fish-tail flame invented, a gasolier might hang from the ceiling, its fixing point surrounded by an oval or circular ceiling rose, which itself became an essential feature in a tasteful room. The cornice, if ornamented, usually

carried a repeated motif of Greek origin, such as acanthus leaf, water leaf or egg-and-dart; and the flat of the ceiling a running low-relief design of anthemion (Greek honeysuckle) or leaves and fruit. In this period there was a shortlived fad for blue-and-white 'clouded' ceilings, though white was commonest from the later eighteenth century onwards. Papier mâché ornaments for ceilings, though often elaborate, were light enough to be fixed in place with screws, a simple process that gave an unexpectedly effective result that was much admired. Ornaments and mouldings have too often been repainted over the years with successive coats of distemper, and these have blotted out their detail; however, dramatic restorations are possible with painstaking paint-stripping and cleaning.

Staircases

In Palladian houses built for wealthy clients in Britain and America, the staircase was often the most impressive feature of the entrance, indeed of the whole interior. In such ambitious houses of the early Georgian period, the entrance lobby and the staircase hall could be of the same width, together forming one rectangular hall the depth of the house. The attic storey would be reached from the first floor by a staircase from a side corridor between front and back rooms and connecting with the staircase from the ground passage. The steps themselves might be open string or closed string, that is, with the tread ends exposed or hidden by an architrave. The stairs were bordered by fine wooden balusters and a sturdy handrail, and the whole made of

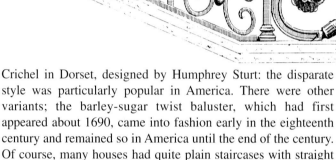

oak, mahogany or, less expensively, pine, in which case the wood was always painted. In open string staircases, exquisite and detailed carving was often given to the tread ends, which could be seen and admired by passers-by.

A common baluster design was the Doric column resting on an urn, with one or two intervening squared blocks. Later, columns became longer and slimmer; as well as being straight-sided, they could be twisted. In this period, variety was obtained by placing three balusters on each tread, in some cases uniform, in other cases each of a different turning, as for example at

Crichel in Dorset, designed by Humphrey Sturt: the disparate style was particularly popular in America. There were other variants; the barley-sugar twist baluster, which had first appeared about 1690, came into fashion early in the eighteenth century and remained so in America until the end of the century. Of course, many houses had quite plain staircases with straight sticks and little or no carved decoration.

Gothic styles of staircase also occurred. Horace Walpole had one installed in Strawberry Hill, Middlesex, describing the work when it was still in hand in 1753: 'Mr Chute and I are come hither for a day or two to inspect the progress of a Gothic staircase which is so pretty and so small that I am inclined to wrap it up and send it to you in my letter.' At every corner of the fretwork balustrade was a modelled antelope holding a shield. That staircase, when finished in 1754, cost £789 2s.

The lower end of the handrail usually terminated as a capping to a newel post, which as a rule was not allowed to project above the rail. A Corinthian-capitalled column for the newel was not uncommon. In the later Georgian period, newel posts were dispensed with and the handrail might sweep round in a bold volute supported by a cluster of balusters that rested on bull-nosed treads at the foot of the staircase. The handrail, even in lesser houses, often swept upwards in a steep curve (a 'ramped' handrail).

In the mid-eighteenth century, staircases continued generally to be in straight flights with landings, but the balusters were usually uniform and slighter and simpler than before.

In the most fashionable homes of the 1750s 'Chinese' fretwork, now known as 'Chinese Chippendale', replaced the balusters. The Adam style, particularly influential from about 1780 to 1800, emphasised curved interiors, and consequently staircase halls were sometimes curved with landings topped by an arch.

By the turn of the century, turned wooden balusters had gone out of style in town houses; instead, thin, square-section stick balusters carrying a narrow handrail were popular. Iron balustrading had become popular in important houses, both town and country. Adam-style balustrades were of graceful design, with patterns based on the lyre, the letter 'S', a vase shape or the anthemion. Robert Adam disliked wooden balustrading and chose cast iron supplied by the Carron Company, founded near Falkirk in 1760, or wrought iron made by Alexander and Shrimpton, London. In the 1770s, Adam's rival James Wyatt remodelled Heaton Park in Lancashire, installing a staircase of which the wrought-iron handrail is the salient feature, enhanced by beautiful tripods that break the line on the landings and form the bases of tall candlestick shafts. Increasing elegance and economy of space were achieved by the use of stairs that were more and more a continuous curve. Iron balustrading had prompted the invention of the geometric stair, enclosed in an ellipse or half-ellipse, depending on whether the staircase had one flight or two. Geometric staircases comprise stone steps (marble in mansions), an iron balustrade and a curved handrail. The steps are not parallel, all of them being winders, and each one is housed in the wall and rests on the step below, which supports it. Even treads and risers were sometimes made of iron by the turn of the nineteenth century.

OPPOSITE PAGE: *Georgian staircases with elaborate iron openwork, ending in a scroll on the bottom step.*

THIS PAGE: *Turned wooden balusters and carved handrails curving around the newel post. Two or even three balusters to a tread were popular throughout the eighteenth century.*

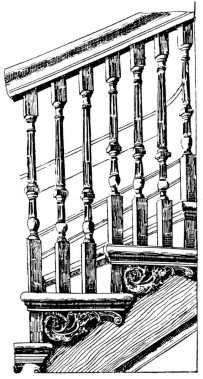

THIS PAGE: *Very decorative wrought-iron balusters embellish these staircases.*

LEFT AND BELOW: *Chandeliers can look splendid – the grandest were called 'lustres' – but the light the original ones afforded was often inadequate. The example on the left hangs in the Palladio Room at Clandon Park, Surrey, which also features a marble fireplace and French flock wallpaper from 1780.*

Lighting

Through most of the Georgian period, homes were lit either by candles or by gas lamps, and in most cases the lighting arrangements were far more aesthetically pleasing than they were satisfactorily functional. In general, candles were held in wall-mounted sconces, in candelabra and chandeliers, in lanterns which could be suspended, affixed to a wall or carried, on shafts set on tripods incorporated into handrails or, more simply, on pedestals. Although tripods or candles can, in sufficient numbers and if well arranged, give out substantial quantities of both heat and light, Georgian houses in America and Britain were, by modern standards, seriously underlit.

Rush lights – dried rushes dipped in animal fat – were the simplest form of candle in the early Georgian period. An alternative used on the north-eastern coast of America was 'candle-wood' – pitch-pine, cut into rough candle shapes. Tallow made from rendered animal fat was another source, but it was more laborious to produce and smelly. It was moulded into candle shapes or a wick was dipped into hot tallow. Tallow lights were among the cheapest options, although William Cobbett noted in 1822 that even these were considered too expensive for

labourers' homes and *Building News* in 1888 still remarked that 'one lamp serves for the house', though by this time the parsimonious house-owner was generally using an oil or paraffin lamp. Where whaling was a significant industry, as for example in New England, spermaceti – a fatty substance from the head of the sperm-whale – could be used for lighting like tallow, either by shaping it into candle form or by dipping a wick into the melted fat, although it gave a better light than tallow.

Beeswax was a still more costly option, affordable only by the wealthy, although it had the advantages of smelling less and giving off less smoke. Beeswax of suitable quality was not produced in either America or in Britain and had to be imported. Beeswax candles were often dyed red, yellow, black or, especially in America, green. In the early nineteenth century, the development of a wax-hardening process enabled candles to burn more steadily and with less mess, and as a result candles continued to be a popular choice.

Candle-holders in the early eighteenth century tended to be sturdy objects generally made of brass or of bronze, and designed to hold one or more candles. Earlier, candle clips or holders were crude iron or tin devices. In the mid-eighteenth century, the fashion was for slim, elegant candlesticks, made of silver, pewter, glass or porcelain and designed along clean, unfussy lines. After about 1760 the fluted stick, with perhaps a palm-leaf or Corinthian capital and a foot in the shape of a dome or a pyramid, became the most common form. Later in the century, more solid-looking sticks came back into fashion, now made of sheet iron or burnished steel; but the most popular form at that time was the ceramic candlestick. Ceramics were cheaper to buy and easier to maintain than metals, and thanks to technological innovations, could be fashioned into intricate and attractive designs.

Pendant light fittings came in a range of styles, from bowl-shaped brass candelabra with curved and branching candle-holders, to the most massive, elaborate chandeliers, sometimes appropriately called 'lustres', that were hung in rooms of substance such as ballrooms and drawing rooms.

To supplement the light of a chandelier, sconces with highly ornamental backs held candles. They were often fixed in front of mirrors, especially the convex circular mirrors that were so widely available from the 1760s, in order to maximise the distribution of light.

In less wealthy homes, rush tapers were common. They stood in stands that had tripod, round or square bases, and scissors were attached for snuffing out the tapers.

Oil lamps were not much used in the eighteenth century in Britain, being not only unreliable, dirty and smoky, but also dangerous, as the common combination of turpentine and alcohol was highly combustible. On the eastern seaboard of America, however, whale-oil lamps were in widespread use by 1750. A new design of lamp patented by Francois-Pierre Aimé Argand in 1783 became very popular. George Washington's home numbered several Argand lamps in 1800, and by 1820 most homes boasted a few. Known in Britain as a colza-oil lamp in reference to the rapeseed oil it burnt, it provided ten to twelve times as much light as a single candle. Other devices were patented in the early nineteenth century, not least the safety match in 1824, making for increasingly sophisticated lighting.

Coal-gas was first installed in a private home in 1787 and a gaslight was patented in 1799. By the mid-1820s, gas was being supplied to thousands of domestic and street lamps in London alone. Gas street lighting was first installed in America in Baltimore in 1817. Gas did have drawbacks: it posed the danger of explosions, as well as being smelly and dirty; nevertheless, it vastly improved on candle or oil lamps, giving between five and ten times more light than tallow candles. The brightness of gaslights was not adjustable, so numbers of them had to be installed; but on the other hand, they could be fixed in every room, thus avoiding the need to transport lights around the house. Mineral oils such as paraffin did not become available until the 1860s, and electricity in the 1880s.

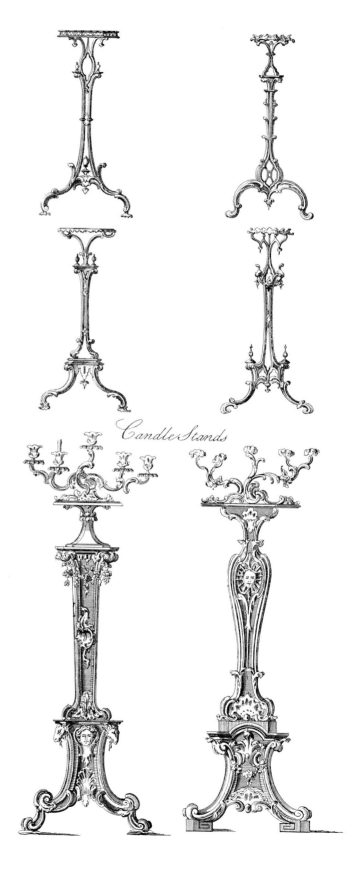

Candle Stands

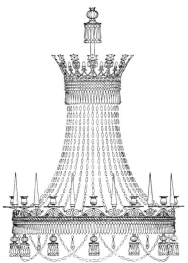

THIS PAGE AND OPPOSITE: *A range of light fittings of various degrees of elaborateness from pattern books of the period. Through most of the Georgian period homes were lit either by candles or by gas lamps, and in most cases the lighting arrangements were far more aesthetically pleasing than they were functional; houses in both America and Britain were, by modern standards, seriously underlit.*

THIS PAGE: *From the 1720s the 'stove grate' was gradually replaced by the 'hob grate'. Both consisted of a free-standing, rectangular basket with fire bars and a grid for falling ash at the bottom, but the hob grate had flat-topped hobs flanking the basket. The chimneypieces on this page display many splendid Georgian features, including marble inset, keystone, fluted pilasters and stylish fireplace furniture. At top right is an example from Williamsberg, Virginia, USA.*

Fireplaces and Chimneypieces

During the early Georgian period, the chimneypiece with shouldered architrave around the fireplace, which had first appeared in Queen Anne's reign, remained in favour, but with variations such as inverted scrolls at the side of a central keystone or tablet. Perhaps the most characteristic chimneypiece of the period had side pilasters, with consoles under the cornice. By the late 1740s Rococo designs had begun to appear, although their flamboyance proved generally too much for British tastes.

William Chambers, appointed in 1760 as one of two joint architects to the Office of Works, the other being his great rival

LEFT: *An Adam-style mantelpiece incorporating* Bossi *work: white marble, carved out and infilled with decorative, coloured marble. The club fender provides additional seating for more relaxed gatherings by this otherwise formal fireside.*

BELOW AND BOTTOM : *The Coalbrookdale or Carron Company, of which John Adam was a partner, manufactured cast-iron surrounds, grates, fenders and fire-irons.*

Robert Adam, published in 1759 his *Treatise on Civil Architecture*, which laid down, *inter alia*, rules for the construction of chimneypieces, including advice on their proportion, location, materials and decoration. Chambers's interiors were normally deliberately sparse, with the focus of his refined ornamentations on ceiling canopies and richly sculptured chimneypieces. In his treatise he wrote:

England is at present possessed of many able sculptors whose chief employment being to execute magnificent chimneypieces, now happily much in vogue, it may be said that in this particular we surpass all other nations.

Chimneypieces by Robert Adam in the later eighteenth century were complete one-storey compositions. The mantelshelf was wider than before and was supported by figure sculpture, pillars terminating in a bust or a caryatid, pilasters without consoles or, more rarely, by columns. Preferred materials in important rooms of stately residences were white marble alone, white and coloured marbles or white marble inlaid with coloured marbles. Adam chimneypieces generally featured a central plaque on the frieze, with a figure, a festoon or some other ornament distinguishing it from the rest of the frieze. For the overmantel a large mirror in a light gilt frame was favoured, although the panel was sometimes decorated by a painting. In great Adam houses such as Harewood and Kenwood, paintings of classical subjects were executed by the particularly sought-after pair of the Italian Antion Zucchi and his wife Angelica Kauffmann. In more modest surroundings, Adam-style chimneypieces were often made in wood and painted. The ornament was generally cast or modelled in composition before being applied.

In America the Greek Revival style, often executed in wood and intricately carved, was popular in the early nineteenth century until about 1840, when simpler geometric surrounds began to be preferred. A slightly raised hearth was a typical feature of American fireplaces.

The trend towards simplicity continued into the Regency period, when the chimneypiece became plain and rectilinear. In some examples the only ornament was on the corner pieces and consisted of a disc of concentric indents, or a plain square, or oblong with shaped corners. Recessed reeding might be found at the sides. For the best rooms marble was used or coloured scagliola, made from coloured plaster and aggregates moulded to resemble marble and capable of receiving a high polish. Gothic designs were revived in the 1820s, featuring lively embellishments.

In the late Georgian period, cheaper chimneypieces were usually made of plaster or painted pine, although by 1830, cast-iron fireplaces were very prevalent, often decorated with patterned tiles. Tin-glazed 'Delft' tiles were commonly imported from Holland in the first half of the eighteenth century, but by 1750 were being usurped by tiles of British manufacture. For a time, about 1790, wallpaper took the place of tiles altogether, until a revival of tile-making occurred at the very end of the Georgian period. 'Coade stone', in fact a highly durable ceramic, came on the market by the turn of the nineteenth century.

When wood was the fuel, firedogs or andirons were used to support logs. As coal was increasingly used, the fireplace opening became smaller; in old, wide hearths the stove grate was a free-standing, rectangular basket for holding the coals. In the new houses, cast-iron, coal-burning hob grates were installed, consisting of a basket flanked by flat-topped hobs on which pots and kettles could be kept warm. No longer freestanding, these cast-iron grates were fixed and took up the whole width of the new narrower fireplace. The front of a hob grate was patterned with classical motifs and its sides curved into an urn shape. An engraved serpentine front and tall finials were typical of early eighteenth-century grates.

Chimney Piece

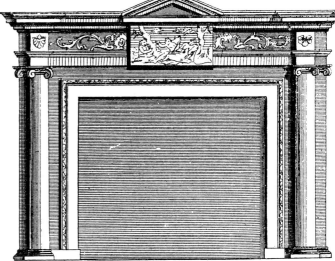

THIS PAGE AND OPPOSITE: *Two stove grates (left) for burning logs, and a selection of chimneypieces. As the Georgian period wore on, chimneypieces, once very ornate and decorated with bucolic scenes, began to develop along simpler, more Classical lines.*

Chapter 5
The Garden

'The works of a person that builds, begin immediately to decay; while those of him who plants begin directly to improve.'

William Shenstone (1714–63), Unconnected Thoughts on Gardening, *1764*

When the Georgian period opened, the English garden still clung to its antecedents. There was the Tudor-style knot garden, in which plantings in raised beds formed regular patterns; the formal French garden of wide walks and sweeping panoramic views, with parterres or broderies, areas of flowing patterns that fitted into the grand scheme, and parcels of woodland called boskets (or *bosquets*), often entirely formal and symmetrical; and Dutch-style gardens with fountains and an abundance of topiary work. These were all swept away, in many cases forever, in the early eighteenth century when informality became the craze, or specifically when, as Horace Walpole put it, in *The History of the Modern Taste in Gardening*, 1771–80):

At that moment appeared [William] Kent [?1685–1748], painter enough to taste the charms of landscape, bold and opinionative enough to dare and to dictate, and born with a genius to strike out a great system from the twilight of imperfect essays. He leaped the fence, and saw that all nature was a garden.

William Kent's first great work was at Chiswick, London, for Lord Burlington, where the villa was set in a large garden, the first in England to be designed on the principle of creating a kind of informality by improving the natural environment. The repertory of Kent and his contemporaries Charles Bridgeman (d.1738) and James Gibbs (1682–1754) included serpentine walks and watercourses, Classical or Gothick temples, statues, obelisks and follies, and the ha-ha, a sunken ditch that served as a barrier to animals without disrupting the view.

At Stowe was probably the richest array of temples and garden ornaments of any contemporary garden; the garden itself was the most important of the period, having been conceived and

OPPOSITE PAGE: *An informal garden of the kind early Georgian gardeners tried to achieve by 'improving' the natural environment, with ornamental lakes and waterways and careful plantings of trees.*

ABOVE: *Eighteenth-century garden designers such as William Kent, Charles Bridgeman and James Gibbs would often station eye-catching features – like this Classical-style 'temple' – in the vistas they were aiming to create.*

essentially determined by Bridgeman, Gibbs, Kent and Sir John Vanbrugh. It was here, too, that Lancelot Brown (1716–83), later nicknamed 'Capability' from his habit of referring to the 'capabilities' of sites on which he was consulted, came to work in March 1741, and stayed as head gardener for ten years. Influenced at first by Kent's manner, Brown soon evolved a simpler and more precise style, which specified conifers and deciduous trees.

Brown's new and radical style was one of the three dominant gardening themes of the second half of the eighteenth century, the others being Orientalism and the emergence of and debate about the Picturesque style. Characteristic Brownian elements were generous plantations flanking the house to screen domestic quarters and stables; the elimination of buildings, statues, mottoes and inscriptions in the garden; a lawn sweeping up to the walls of the house, uninterrupted by terraces; a winding drive offering glimpses of the house between trees; sinuous outlines of water; an encircling ride or shelter belt; and trees in scattered clumps or single specimens on lawns at the back or front of the house. Brown's predilection for the natural made him do away with such formality as he found and to conceal purely utilitarian features. Few of his plans or drawings survive, however, although his name is connected (in legend if not in fact) with about two hundred estates in England.

William Chambers (1723–96) had, unlike most of his contemporaries, actually visited China, and he drew on his experiences to create Chinese styles in gardens, notably at Kew, London, where he claimed he had, with the famous Pagoda and other Chinese elements, made an Eden out of 'what was once a Desart'. Other English writers, such as William Halfpenny (fl.1723–55) and his son John, promoted the Chinese taste in such books as *Rural Architecture in the Chinese Taste* (1750), *New Designs for Chinese Temples (1750)* – the first book of Chinese designs to be published in England – and *Chinese and Gothic Architecture Properly Ornamented*. William Halfpenny was indeed the most prolific author of architectural books of his time, and twelve of his twenty-two books are known to have been available in the American colonies before 1776.

Brown's principles were continued, with adaptations, by his almost equally famous successor, Humphrey Repton (1752–1818). Repton differed from Brown, however, perhaps most markedly in favouring a more practical approach to the relationship between house and garden, that prefigured the Picturesque movement. The notion sat comfortably with the eminent architect John Nash (1752–1835), who was Repton's partner from about 1795 to 1802. Brown's houses, with their lawns swirling right up to their walls, stood out from their surroundings, as though on a pedestal or an island. Repton's houses, by contrast, merged into the landscape.

The Picturesque debate of the 1790s was led by Richard Payne Knight (1750–1824) and Sir Uvedale Price (1747–1829),

and was founded partly out of the ideas of the Rev. William Gilpin (1724–1804). Initially the idea of picturesqueness came out of the siting of country houses or of ornamental buildings in romantic settings such as in groves or beside lakes. In landscaping the term first meant 'like a picture', specifically recalling the landscape paintings of Claude Lorrain, Rosa and Poussin; later it came to mean free and vigorous, and involving a greater respect for raw nature than Brownian style, which was rejected as bland and insipid. According to Price, 'the two opposite qualities of roughness, and of sudden variation, joined to that of irregularity, are the most efficient causes of the picturesque'. Picturesqueness was, to him, a quality *per se*, to be preserved and enhanced. Price, who had a fondness for categorisation, even drew up tables of objects to indicate their level of picturesqueness: thus cultivated countryside was dismissed as unpicturesque; ruins and hovels were more picturesque than cottages; cows more than horses; vagrants and idlers more than labouring people, and so on.

The English landscape garden had become internationally renowned and copied – regardless of its suitability to terrain or climate – in Scotland and Ireland, in continental Europe, in Russia, and in the United States, where Washington's and Jefferson's homes at Mount Vernon and Monticello respectively benefited from English examples.

John Nash, perhaps most famously, brought gardens into an urban environment, ingeniously blending a 'natural' landscape in the Picturesque mode into a monumental scheme of formal Classical terraces and individual villas in parkland.

In cities and towns, gardens were rare until the advent of suburbanisation in the early nineteenth century. The larger London squares in the seventeenth century were laid out at first in the precise and regular manner of the Renaissance garden, but later, in the eighteenth century, were turned into miniature landscaped gardens. The better terraces gave out onto such a square or garden, often called a 'paddock' in London or, in Brighton, an 'enclosure'. Alternatively, a strip of greenery might be laid down between the street and the private driveway in front of the houses. Until the mid-nineteenth century, the rear of the house in most places was associated with 'service', not with family use, and back gardens were thus not much cultivated, in

BELOW: *In the late eighteenth century Coade stone was widely adopted for making garden ornaments as it was hard and durable, and was frost-resistant.*

BOTTOM LEFT: *Sir Uvedale Price (1747–1829), an advocate of the Picturesque movement, drew up tables of levels of picturesqueness – for instance, ruins were considered more picturesque than cottages.*

BELOW: *This conservatory would afford attractive views from within as well as making a pretty addition to the house when seen from the garden.*
OAK LEAF CONSERVATORIES

BOTTOM RIGHT: *In many great gardens of the early eighteenth century, avenues of trees were trained by pleaching (tying new growths to horizontal wires attached to tall poles).*

LEFT: *A ha-ha, a sunken ditch that served as an effective barrier to animals but did not disrupt the vista.*

BELOW LEFT: *A stone urn at the junction of paths sets off the lawn on one side and the massed plantings on the other.*

BELOW: *Statues were not merely decorative but, with their Classical allusions, were intended to have intellectual appeal to people of education and discernment.*

either sense. Exceptionally, the main entrance to terraced houses was at the back, and the front was endowed with ample greenery so as to give continuity with parkland or an unobstructed view. Humphrey Repton and others of his generation, such as John Britton, believed that direct access to a garden from the house was desirable and that main living rooms should therefore be placed on the ground floor.

In England in the nineteenth century massed planting became popular, featuring plants arranged perhaps by colour, by season of flowering, or by type, such as bulbs or annuals. In 1804 explorations revealed previously little known parts of North America to be rich sources for botanists. The Horticultural Society of London took an interest and sent out David Douglas, who on his extensive travels between 1823 and 1834, collected and sent back to England a huge assortment of trees, shrubs and other plants. Mexico and the Himalayas were further sources of species that were planted in English pleasure grounds or arboreta, often in areas specially set aside for them. Australasian plants, introduced at the end of the eighteenth century, were

generally grown under glass or scattered throughout gardens, rather than in designated areas. The range of plants available from around the world was by this time becoming so wide that private gardeners had of necessity to concentrate on a particular area of garden or a certain type of plant.

In many great gardens of the late seventeenth and early eighteenth centuries, avenues of trees were trimmed flat to create long vistas, or trees were trained by pollarding (cutting off the upper branches), pruning or pleaching (tying new growths to horizontal wires attached to tall poles); or they might be trained over metal supports to form a tunnel or arbour.

On garden paths in the seventeenth and eighteenth centuries pebble mosaics were popular, although very laborious to make. Paths themselves were sometimes made of creeping plants such as thyme, chamomile or creeping mint. For path edgings in formal gardens of the seventeenth century, *Buxus sempervirens* (dwarf box) was used. The ribbon walk and the winding path of the early eighteenth century were edged with wooden boards. Later still, formal stone edging was used for flower gardens.

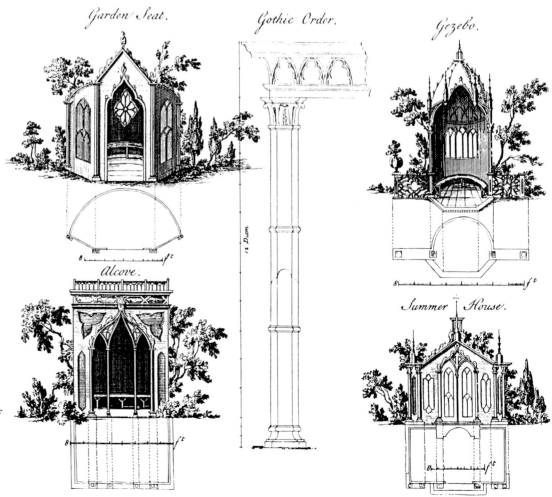

THIS PAGE: *Designs for garden buildings, all in the Gothick style (the Regency adaptation of Gothic). By this period, the main reason behind their creation was more to surprise and amuse than to provide sensible garden rooms.*

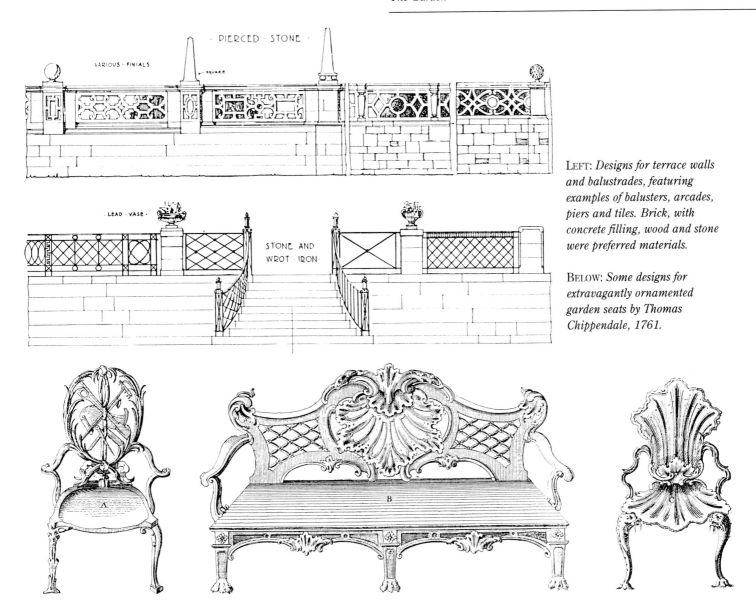

LEFT: *Designs for terrace walls and balustrades, featuring examples of balusters, arcades, piers and tiles. Brick, with concrete filling, wood and stone were preferred materials.*

BELOW: *Some designs for extravagantly ornamented garden seats by Thomas Chippendale, 1761.*

Garden furniture, such as seats, chairs and tables, was made in styles such as were recommended in the numerous pattern books of the period, and that matched interior furniture and indeed the architecture of the main building: thus seats and chairs came in Classical, chinoiserie, Gothick and neo-Classical styles. Materials were, at first, oak or a similar hardwood, or larch, yew, apple or pear; and, later, wrought iron, always painted to give protection against rust.

Orangeries, which served to protect orange trees in winter, were in their earliest forms rather like other garden buildings, with tiled roofs; towards the end of the eighteenth century, the realisation that light was beneficial to plants led to their substitution with glazed roofs. Flues under the floors and in the walls conveyed heat from an outside furnace. Overall glazing became more common with the introduction of plants such as pelargoniums that demanded a lot of light. In the nineteenth century many houses incorporated conservatories entered directly from the house. Other garden buildings included neo-Classical temples (such as the Rotunda at Stowe) and pavilions. Designs for decorative chinoiserie buildings, such as pagodas, mostly of brightly painted, lacquered and gilt timber, could be found in pattern books by Chambers, Halfpenny or in Charles Over's *Ornamental Architecture in the Gothic, Chinese and Modern Taste* (1758). Incidentally, pattern books also suggested ideas for tubs and window-boxes for people without gardens, although from the mid-eighteenth century plants and gardening were a passion among the middle and upper classes.

STOCKISTS

The lists of suppliers given on these pages cannot be exhaustive and are intended only as a starting point. Local papers and commercial telephone directories are always worth looking at and are good sources of information about your own area. Alternatively there are many organisations giving specialist information and advice, and others who will search for specific items.

UNITED KINGDOM
INFORMATION AND ADVICE

Architectural Salvage
Netley House
Gomshall
Surrey GU5 2QA
Tel: 0148 641 3221
Index of architectural items. For a fee of £10 they will put buyers in touch with sellers. They do not keep items for sale.

The Brooking Collection
Woodhay, White Lane
Guildford
Surrey GU4 8PU
Tel: 01483 504555
Unique record of the development of period detail. Information and advice available.

English Heritage
25 Savile Row
London W1X 2BT
Tel: 0171 734 6010
Provides specialist and technical advice on repair, maintenance and preservation; also gives grants for repairing historic buildings throughout England.

The Georgian Group
76 Fitzroy Square
London W1P 6DX
Tel: 0171 387 1720
Gives advice on repair and restoration to owners of Georgian buildings.

The Guild of Master
Craftsmen
166 High Street Lewes
East Sussex
Tel: 01273 477374
Trade association putting prospective clients in touch with experienced craftsmen able to carry out restoration work. Also publishes Guide to Restoration Experts.

The Society for the
Protection of Ancient
Buildings
37 Spital Square
London E1 6DY
Tel: 0171 377 1644
Issues technical publications on historic buildings repairs and can supply names of specialist architects and other professionals.

ARCHITECTURAL ANTIQUES
AND REPRODUCTIONS

Architectural Antiques
70 Penbroke Street
Bedford MK40 3RQ
Tel: 01234 213131

Architectural Rescue
1–3 Southampton Way
Camberwell
London SE5 7JH
Tel: 0171 277 0315

Bailey's Architectural
Antiques
The Engine Shed
Ashburton Industrial Estate
Ross-on-Wye
Herefordshire HE9 7BW
Tel: 0989 63015

Brighton Architectural
Salvage
33–44 Gloucester Road
Brighton BN1 4AQ
Tel: 01273 681656

Britain's Heritage
Shaftesbury Hall
3 Holy Bones
Leicester
Tel: 0116 2519592

Cranbourne Stone
West Orchard
Shaftesbury
Dorset SP7 0LJ
Tel: 01258 472685

D. & P. Theodore
Reclamation First
North Road
Bridgend Industrial Estate
Bridgend, mid-Glamorgan
Tel: 01656 648936

Edinburgh & Glasgow
Architectural Salvage
Yards
Unit 6 Gouper Street
Edinburgh
Tel: 0131 554 7077

Haddonstone
The Forge House
East Haddon
Northampton NN6 8DB
Tel: 01604 770711

Shiners
123 Jesmond Road
Jesmond
Newcastle-upon-Tyne
Tel: 0191 281 6474

Solopark Ltd
The Old Railway Station
Station Road,
near Pampisford
Cambridgeshire CB2 4HB
Tel: 01223 834663

Walcot Reclamation
108 Walcot Street
Bath
Avon BA1 5BG
Tel: 01225 444404

Warehouse Antiques
17 Wilton Street
Holderness Road
Hull
Tel: 01482 326559

CONSERVATORIES
Amdega Ltd
Faverdale, Darlington
Co Durham DL3 0PW
Tel: 01325 468522

Goldcrest Conservatories
Woolners Way
Stevenage
Herts SG1 3AF
Tel: 01438 361671

Classical Conservatories
Unit 16c
Chalwyn Industrial Estate
St Clements Road
Poole
Dorset BH15 3PE
Tel: 01202 733001

Malbrook Conservatories
2 Keswick Road
London SW15 2 JL
Tel: 0181 875 1441

Oak Leaf Conservatories
Ltd
Kettlestring Lane
Clifton Common
York YO3 4XF
Tel: 01904 690 401

Vale Garden Houses
Melton Road
Harlaxton, Nr Grantham
Lincolnshire NG32 1HQ
Tel: 01476 64433

DOORS & WINDOWS
Copycats
The Workshop
29 Maypole Road
Ashurst Wood
West Sussex RH17 IJA

Fineline Traditional Joinery
Honeybridge Mushroom
Farm
Honeybridge Lane
Dial Post, Horsham
West Sussex RH13 8NX
Tel: 01402 711530

Indoors Ltd
Invicta Works, Mill St
East Malling
Tel: 01732 841606

The London Door
Company
153 St John's Hill
London SW11 1TQ
Tel: 0800 387 905

Parke and Sestini
The Old Engine House
Hall Farm, Main Street
Kirklington
Newark
Notts NG22 8NN
Tel: 01636 816415

Restoration Windows
25 Marlborough Crescent
Bedford Park
London W4 IHE

The Sash Window
Workshop
Unit 2, Mayfield Farm
Industrial Estate
Hatchet Lane, Cranbourne,
Windsor
Berkshire SL4 2EG

Henry Venables Ltd
Doxey Road
Stafford ST16 2EN
Tel: 01785 215087

DOOR FURNITURE
Architectural Components
Ltd
4–8 Exhibition Road
London SW7 2HF
Tel: 0171 581 2401

Beardmore Architectural
Ironmongery
3–4 Percy Street
London W1P OEJ
Tel: 0171 637 7041

Brass Tacks Hardware Ltd
177 Bilton Road
Perivale, Greenford
Middlesex
Tel: 0181 566 9669

Clayton-Munroe
Kingston, Staverton
Totnes
Devon TQ9 6AR
Tel: 01803 762626

The Empire & Colonial
Knocker Company
PO Box 1876, Tamworth
Staffs B77 4RY
Tel: 01827 56454

The Fingerplate Company
1 Golygfa Dwyrain
Llandw, Cowbridge
Sth Glamorgan
CF71 7NZ
Tel: 01656 890691

The Period House Group
Main Street
Leavening
N Yorks YO17 9SA
Tel: 01653 658554

FABRICS AND WALLPAPERS

Alexander Beauchamp
2/12 Second Floor
Chelsea Harbour Design
    Centre
Chelsea Harbour
London SW10 0XE
Tel: 0171 376 4556

Cole & Son
142–4 Offord Road
London N1 1NS
Tel: 0171 607 4288

Colefax and Fowler
39 Brook Street
London W1Y 2JE
Tel: 0171 493 2231

Hamilton Weston
    Wallpapers Ltd
18 St Mary's Grove
Richmond
Surrey TW9 1UY
Tel: 0181 940 4850

Ornamenta
Old Chelsea Mews
Danvers Street
London SW3 5AN
Tel: 0171 352 1824

Sanderson & Sons
112–120 Brompton Road
London SW3 1JJ
Tel: 0171 584 3344

Zoffany
63 South Audley Street
London W1 5BS
Tel: 0171 495 2505

FIREPLACES

Antique Fireplace Centre
30 Molesworth Road
Millbridge
Plymouth
Tel: 01752 559441

Antique Fireplace
    Warehouse
194–202 Battersea Park Road
London SW11 4ND
Tel: 0171 627 1410

Ashburton Marbles
6 West Street, Ashburton
Devon TQ13 7DU
Tel: 01364 53189

Chiswick Fireplace Company
68 Southfield Road
Chiswick
London W4
Tel: 0181 995 4011

Club Fenders from
    Acres Farm
Bradfield
Berkshire, RG7 6JH
Tel: 01734 744305

Coalbrookdale
Glynwed Consumer &
    Building Products Ltd
PO Box 30 Ketley
Telford
Shropshire TF1 1BR
Tel: 01952 51177

James Gray & Sons Ltd
89 George Street
Edinburgh EH2 3EZ
Tel: 0131 225 7381

Marble Hill Fireplaces Ltd
72 Richmond Road
Twickenham
Middlesex TW1 3BE
Tel: 0171 892 1488

Jonathan Murray Fireplaces
358 Upper Richmond Road
West East Sheen
London SW14 7JT
Tel: 0181 876 7934

The Original Architectural
    Heritage of Cheltenham
Boddington Manor
Boddington, Nr Cheltenham
Gloucestershire GL51 0TJ
Tel: 012426 8741

Rockingham Fender Seats
Grange Farm,
Thorney
Peterborough PE6 0PJ
Tel: 01733 270233

Townsends
81 Abbey Road
London NW8 0AE
Tel: 0171 624 4756

KITCHENS

Bygone Ltd
Fieldside Farm, Quainton
Aylesbury
Bucks HP22 4DQ
Tel: 0296 655573

Bylaw The Furniture
    Makers
Bylaw (Ross) Ltd
The Old Mill,
Brookend Street
Ross-on-Wye
Herefordshire HR9 7EG
Tel: 01989 562356

Chalon UK Ltd
Hambridge Mill
Hambridge
Somerset TA10 0BP
Tel: 01458 252374

Naturally Wood
Twyford Road
Bishops Stortford
Hertfordshire
CM23 3JL
Tel: 01279 755501

Newcastle Furniture
    Company
Green Lane Buildings
Pelaw, Tyne & Wear
NE10 0UW
Tel: 0191 438 1342

Robinson & Cornish
Southay House
Oakwood Close, Barnstaple
Devon EX31 3NJ
Tel: 01271 329300

Mark Wilkinson Furniture Ltd
Overton House
High Street, Bromham
Chippenham
Wiltshire SN15 2HA
Tel: 01380 850004

Smallbone of Devizes
Showrooms:
London, Devizes, Harrogate,
Leamington Spa,
Tunbridge Wells
Tel: 0171 589 5998

KITCHEN RANGES

Aga-Rayburn
PO Box 30, Ketley, Telford
Shropshire TF1 4DD
Aga Tel: 0345 125207
Rayburn Tel: 0345 626147

Alpha Cookers (UK)
89 New Greenham Park
Greenham, Thatcham
Berkshire RG19 6HW
Tel: 01635 582068

Architectural Heritage
The Woodyard
A5 Brockhall, Weedon
Northants NN7 4LB
Tel: 01 327 349349

Country Cookers
Bruff Works, Bushbank
Suckley
Worcestershire WR6 5DR
Tel: 01886 884262

Wye Valley Stoves &
    Fireplaces
Station Street, Ross-on-Wye
Herefordshire HR9 7AG
Tel: 01989 565870

Yorkshire Range Company
Japonica, Church Lane
Halton East, Skipton
North Yorkshire BD23 6EH
Tel: 01756 710263

LIGHTING

Best & Lloyd Ltd
William Street West
Smethwick
Warley
West Midlands B66 2NX
Tel: 0121 558 1191

R. & J. Chelsom & Co Ltd
Squires Gate Industrial
    Estate
Blackpool
Lancashire FY4 3RN
Tel: 01253 46324

Lights on Broadway
Showrooms:
Fulham, Camden,
Greenwich, Brighton
Tel: 0181 453 1656

Magic Lanterns
By George
23 George Street
St Albans, Herts
Tel: 01727 865680

Olivers Lighting Company
6 The Broadway
Crockenhill, Swanley
Kent BR8 8JH
Tel: 01322 614224

Albert Bartram
177 Hivings Hill, Chesham
Bucks HP5 2PN
Tel: 01494 783271

Starlite Chandeliers Ltd
127 Harris Way, Windmill Rd
Sunbury-on-Thames
TW16 7EL
Tel: 019327 88686

Sugg Lighting
65 Gatwick Road, Crawley
Sussex RH10 2YU
Tel: 01293 540111

Wick's End
29 The Business Centre
Bowbridge Close, Rotherham
South Yorkshire S60 1BY
Tel: 01709 843029

Christopher Wray's Lighting
600 Kings Road
London SW6 2DX
Tel: 0171 736 8434

METALWORK

Beardmore & Co Ltd
3–4 Percy Street
London W1P 0EJ
Tel: 0171 637 7041

Bishopbourne Forge
Bishopsbourne
Canterbury CT4 5HT
Tel: 01227 830784

Britannia Architectural
    Metalwork
The Old Coach House
Draymans Way, Alton
Hampshire GU34 1AY
Tel: 01420 84427

Colston Forge
Colston Yard, Colston Street
Bristol BA1 5BD
Tel: 01179 273660

Dorothea Restorations Ltd
New Road, Whaley Bridge
Stockport
Cheshire SK12 7JG
Tel: 01663 733544

George James & Sons Ltd
Cransley Hill, Broughton
Northamptonshire NN14 1NB
Tel: 01536 790295

J.H. Porter & Son Ltd
13 Cranleigh Mews
Cabul Road
London SW11 2QL
Tel: 0171 978 5576

Kentish Ironcraft Ltd
Ashford Road
Bethersden, Ashford
Kent TN26 3AT
Tel: 01233 820805

S. Lunn & Sons
Old School Works
Red Row, Morpeth
Northumberland NE61 5AU
Tel: 01670 760246

MOULDING & PANELLING
Allied Guilds
Unit 19 Reddicap Trading
    Estate, Coleshill Road
Sutton Coldfield
West Midlands B75 7BU
Tel: 0121 329 2874

Aristocast Originals
Bold Street
Sheffield S9 2LR
Tel: 01742 561156

Butcher Plastering
    Specialists Ltd
8 Fitzroy Road
Primrose Hill
London NW1 8TX
Tel: 0181 722 9771/2

Hallidays
Dept PLP. The Old College
Dorchester-on-Thames
Oxon OX10 7HL
Tel: 01865 340028

Locker & Riley
Capital House
Faraday Road, Leigh on Sea
Essex SS9 5JU
Tel: 01702 511661

Renaissance Mouldings
262 Handsworth Road
Handsworth
Sheffield S13 9BS

The Plaster Care Company
2 Churchfield Road
Ealing
London W13 9NG
Tel: 0181 567 5901

John Powson
4 Harsley Walk
Middlesbourough
Cleveland TS3 9PT
Tel: 01642 211201

Stevensons of Norwich
Roundtree Way
Norwich NR7 8SQ
Tel: 01604 400824

Winther Browne & Co Ltd
Nobel Road
Eleys Estate
London N 18 3DX
Tel: 0818 803 3434

PAINTS AND STAINS
Brodie & Middleton
68 Drury Lane
London WC2B 5SP
Tel: 0171 836 3289

Colourman Paints
Pine Brush Products
Coton Clanford
Staffordshire STA18 9PB
Tel: 01785 282799

Cornelissen Ltd
105 Great Russell Street
London WC1B 3RY
Tel: 0171 636 1045

Craig & Rose
172 Leith Walk
Edinburgh
EH6 5EB
Tel: 0131 554 1131

Cy-pres (Brigstock) Ltd
14 Bells Close
Brigstock
Kettering
Northamptonshire
NN14 3JG
Tel: 01536 373431

Dulux Heritage Range
ICI Paints
Wexham Road
Slough SL2 5DS
Tel: 01420 23024

Farrow & Ball Ltd
Uddens Trading Estate
Wimbourne
Dorset BH21 7NL
Tel: 01202 876141

Hirst Conservation
    Material Ltd
Laughton Hall Farmhouse
Laughton, Sleaford
Lincolnshire NG34 OHE
Tel: 015929 497517

John Keep & Sons
Unit 1, The Industrial Site
Croydon Road, Elmers End
Beckenham, Kent
Tel: 01891 658 2299

Keim Mineral Paints Ltd
Muckley Cross
Morville, Bridgnorth
Shropshire WV16 4RR
Tel: 01746 714543

The Lime Centre
Long Barn, Morestead
Winchester
Hampshire SO21 ILZ
Tel: 01962 713636

Ludlow Period House Shop
141 Corve Street
Ludlow SY8 2PG
Tel: 01584 877276

John Oliver Ltd
33 Pembridge Road
London W11 3HG
Tel: 0171 221 6466

Papers & Paints
4 Park Walk
London SW10 OAD
Tel: 0171 352 8626

Potmolen Paint
27 Woodcock Industrial
    Estate, Warminster
Wiltshire BA11 9DX
Tel: 01985 213960

Rose of Jericho
    at St Blaise Ltd
Westhill Barn
Evershot, Dorchester
Dorset DT2 OLD
Tel: 01935 83676

USA
ARCHITECTURAL SALVAGE YARDS
Architectural Antiques
1321 East 2nd
Little Rock, AR72202
Tel: (501) 372–1744

Architectural Salvage
    Warehouse
337 Berry Street
Brooklyn, NY 11211
Tel: 718 388 4527

Great American Salvage Co
34 Cooper Square
New York, NY 10013
Tel: 212 505 0070

Irreplaceable Artifacts
14 Second Avenue at
Houston St
New York, NY 10013
Tel: 212 777 2900

Jerard Paul Jordan Gallery
Slade Acres, PO Box 71
Ashford, CT 06278
Tel: 204 429 7954

Joe Ley Antiques, Inc
615 East Market Street
Louisvill, KY 40202
Tel: 502 583 4014

Material Unlimited
2 West Michigan Avenue
Ypsilanti, MI 48197
Tel: 313 483 6980

Nostalgia Architectural
    Antiques
307 Stiles Avenue
Savannah, GA 31401
Tel: 912 232 2324

United House Wrecking
328 Selleck Street
Stamford, CT 06902
Tel: 203 348 5371

Walker's
PO Box 309
Tallmadge, OH 44278
Tel: 216 6331081

The Wrecking Bar of
    Atlanta Inc
292 Moreland Avenue NE
Atlanta, GA 30307
Tel: (40) 525 0468

COLUMNS
Classic Architectural
    Specialities
5302 Junius
Dallas, TX 75214
Tel: 211 827 5111

Dovetail
Box 1569
Lowell, MA 01853–2796
Tel: 800 344 5570

Haddonstone (USA) Ltd
201 Heller Place, Interstate
Business Park, Bewllmawr
NJ 08031
Tel: 609 931 0040

Haddonstone (USA) Ltd
5362 Industrial Drive,
Huntingdon Beach
CA 92649
Tel: 714 894 3500

Old South Columns
Moultrie Manufacturing
Company, PO Box 1179
Moultrie, GA 31768
Tel: 800 841 8674

Robinson Iron
Robinson Road
Alexander City, AL 35010
Tel: 205 329 8486

A.F. Schwerd
    Manufacturing Co
3215 McClure Avenue
Pittsburgh, PA 15212
Tel: 413 766 6322

CONSERVATORIES
Amdega Centre
160 Friendship Road
Cranbury, NJ 18512
Tel: 201 320 0999

Machin Designs (USA) Inc
652 Glenbrook Road
Stamford, CT 06906
Tel: 203 348 5319

Oak Leaf Conservatories Ltd
876 Davis Drive
Atlanta, GA 30327
Tel: 800 360 6283

DOORS AND WINDOWS
Beech River Mill Company
Old Route 16
Center Ossipee, NH 03814
Tel: 603 539 2636

Blaine Window Hardware Inc
1919 Blaine Drive RD4
Hagerstown, MD 21740
Tel: 301 797 6500

Colonial Restoration
    Products
405 East Walnut Street
North Wales, PA 19454
Tel: 215 699 3133

Historic Windows
PO Box 1172
Harrisonburg, VA 22801
Tel: 703 434 5855

Hope's Architectural
   Products Inc
James Town
NY 14701

Kenmore Industries
1 Thompson Square
PO Box 34
Boston, MA 02129
Tel: 617 242 1711

Marvin Windows
Box 100
Warroad, MN 56763
Tel: 800 346 5128

Materials Unlimited
2 West Michigan Avenue
Ypsilanti, MI 48197
Tel: 313 483 6980

Maurer & Shepherd
   Joyners Inc
122 Naubuc Avenue
Glastonbury, CT 06033
Tel: 203 633 2383

National Door Company
   Inc
5 Summer Place
Saranac Lake, NY 12983
Tel: 518 891 2001

Sheppard Millwork
21020 70th Avenue West
Edmonds, WA 98020
Tel: 206 771 4645

Silverton Mill Works
Box 850–FAA
Silverton, CO 81433
Tel: 303 387 5716

Walker's
PO Box 309
Tallmadge, OH 44278
Tel: 216 633 1081

The Woodstone Company
PO Box 223
Patch Road
Westminster
VT 05158
Tel: 802 722 4784

FABRICS & WALLPAPERS
Laura Ashley
1300 MacArthur Boulevard
Mahwah, NJ 07430
Tel: 201 934 3000

Nancy Borden, Period
   Textile Furnishing
PO Box 4381
Portsmouth, NH 03801
Tel: 603 4367 4284

Brunschwig et Fils
979 Third Avenue
New York, NJ 10022
Tel: 212 838 7878

S.M. Hexter Company
2800 Superior Avenue
Cleveland, OH 44114
Tel: 216 696 0146

Hodsoll McKenzie
Clarence House
211 East 58th Street
New York NY 10022

Lee Jofa
979 Third Avenue
New York, NY 10022
Tel: 212 688 0444

Raintree Designs Inc
979 Third Avenue
New York, NY10022
Tel: 212 477 8590

Scalamandre
24–37 24th Street
Long Island City,
NY 11101
Tel: 212 980 3888

F. Schumacher & Co
939 Third Avenue
New York, NY 10022
Tel: 212 415 3900

FIREPLACES & STOVES
Danny Alessandro Ltd
Edwin Jackson Inc
1156 Second Avenue
New York, NY 10021
Tel: 212 421 1928

Danny Alessandro Ltd
8409 Santa Monica
Boulevard
Los Angeles, CA 90069
Tel: 213 654 6198

Barnstaple Stove Shop
Route 149
PO Box 472
West Barnstaple, MA
02668
Tel: 617 362 9913

Bryant Stove Works
Thorndike, ME 04986
Tel: 207 568 3665

Driwood Molding C
PO Box 1729
Florence, SC 29503–1729
Tel: 803 669 2478

Stephen English
English Fireplaces
1772 Union Street
San Francisco, CA 94123
Tel: 415 775 2164

C.G. Girolami & Co
944–946 N Spaulding Ave
Chicago, IL 60651
Tel: 312 227 1959

Samuel Heath & Sons plc
4600 Highlands Parkway,
Suite J
Smyrna, GA 30080

Nostalgia Architectural
   Antiques
207 Stiles Avenue
Savannah, GA 31401
Tel: 912 232 2324

Old World Molding and
   Finishing Inc
115 Allen Boulevard
Farmingdale, NY 11735
Tel: 516 293 1789

Vermont Structural Slate
   Co Ltd
Box 98, Fair Haven
VT 05743
Tel: 800 343 1900

Virginia Metalcrafters
1010 East Main Street
PO Box 1069
Waynesboro, VA 22980
Tel: 703 949 8205

HARDWARE
Anglo–American Brass Co
4146 Mitzi Drive, Box 9792
San Jose, CA 95157–0792
Tel: 408 246 0203

The Antique Hardware
   Store
43 Bridge Street, Dept PD
Frenchtown, NJ 08825
Tel: 210 996 4040

The Smithy
Wolcott, VT 05680
Tel:802 472 6508

Tremont Nail Company
8 Elm Street, PO Box 111
Wareham, MA 02561
Tel: 617 295 0038

Williamsburg Blacksmiths
Goshen Road
Williamsburg, MA 01096
Tel: 413 268 7341

The Woodbury Blacksmith
   and Forge Co
161 Main Street
PO Box 268
Woodbury, CT 06798
Tel: 203 263 5737

KITCHENS
Allmilmo Corporation
70 Clinton Road
Fairfield, NY 07006

Alno Ltd
109 Wappoo Creek Drive
Suite 43
Charleston, SC 29412
Tel: 803 795 8683

Poggenpohl USA Corp
6 Pearl Court
Allendale, NJ 07401
Tel: 210 934 1511

Siematic Ltd
919 Santa Monica
Boulevard 215
Santa Monica, CA 90401
Tel: 213 395 8394

Smallbone Inc
150 East 58th Street
New York, NY 10022

Winchmore Furniture Ltd
Suite 11, 2695 North
Military Trail
West Palm Beach, FL
33409
Tel: 305 471 7534

LIGHTING
Authentic Designs
The Mill Road
West Rupert, VT 05776
Tel: 802 394 7713

B. & P. Lamp Supply Inc
McMinnville, TN 37110
Tel: 615 473 3016

Ball & Ball
463 W Lincoln Highway
Exton, PA 19341
Tel: 215 363 7330

City Lights
2226 Massachusetts Ave
Cambridge, MA 01240
Tel: 617 547 1490

Classic Lamp Posts
3645 NW 67th Street
Miami, FL 33147

Colonial Metalcrafters
Box 1135
Tyler, TX 75701
Tel: 214 561 1111

A.J.P. Coppersmith & Co
34 Broadway
Wakefield, MA 01880
Tel: 617 245 1223

Hurley Patentee Manor
RD7 Box 98A
Kingston, NY 12401
Tel: 914 331 5414

King's Chandelier CO
Highway 14, PO Box 667
Eden (Leaksville),
NC 27288
Tel: 919 623 6188

Lamp Light
135 Yorkshire Court
Elyria, OH 44035
Tel: 216 365 4954

The London Venturers Co
2 Dock Square
Rockport, MA 01966
Tel: 617 546 7161

Gates Moore
River Road, Silvermine
Norwalk, CT 06850
Tel: 203 847 3231

Paxton Hardware Ltd
7818 Bradshaw Road
Upper Falls
MD 21156
Tel: 301 592 8505

Progress Lighting
Box 12701
Philadelphia
PA 19134–1386
Tel: 215 289 1200

Rejuvenation House Parts
901 N Skidmore
Portland, OR 97217
Tel: 503 249 0774

Renovation Concepts
213 Washington Avenue
North Minneapolic, MN
55401
Tel: 612 333 5766

Roy Electric Co Inc
1054 Coney Island Avenue
Brooklyn, NY 11230
Tel: 718 339 6311

The Saltbox
3004 Columbia Avenue
Lancaster, PA 17603
Tel: 717 392 5649

St Louis Antique
Lighting Co
801 N Skinker
St Louis, MO 63130
Tel: 314 863 1414

Shaker Workshops
PO Box 1028
Concord, MA 01742
Tel: 617 646 8985

Stair & Co Ltd
940 Madison Avenue
New York, NY 10021

Sturbridge Yankee
Workshop
Blueberry Road
Westborrk, ME 04092
Tel: 800 343 1144

Virginia Metalcrafters
PO Box 1068
1010 E Main Street
Waynesboro, VA 22980
Tel: 703 949 8205

METALWORK & FENCING

Architectural Iron
Company
Box 126 Route 6 West
Milford, PA 18337

Cassidy Bros Forge Inc
US Route 1
Rowley, MA 01969–1796
Tel: 617 948 7611

Moultrie Manufacturing Co
PO Drawer 1179
Moultrie, GA 31776–1179
Tel: 800 841 8674

Nostalgia Architectural
Antiques
307 Stiles Avenue
Savannah, GA 31401
Tel: 232 2324

Robinson Iron
Robinson Road
Alexander City, AL 35010
Tel: 205 329 8486

Steel Forge
North Road
Bridgton, ME 04009
Tel: 207 647 8108

Stewart Manufacturing Co
511 Enterprise Drive
Covington, KY 41017
Tel: 606 331 9000

Walpole Woodworkers
767 East Street
Walpole
MA 02081
Tel: 617 668 2800

MOULDING & PANELLING

Bendix Moldings Inc
235 Pegasus Avenue
Northvale, NJ 07647
Tel: 210 767 888

British Plaster Moldings
6395c McDonough Drive
Norcross, GA 30071
Tel: 912 447 5078

Classic Architectural
Specialities
5302 Junius
Dallas, TX 75214
Tel: 214 827 5111

Cumberland Woodcraft
Co Inc
PO Drawer 609
Carlisle, PA 17013
Tel: 717 243 0063

Dovetail
Box 1569
Lowell, MA 01853–2796
Tel: 800 344 5570

Driwood Molding
Company
PO Box 1729
Florence, SC 29503–1729
Tel: 803 669 2478

C.G. Girolami & Company
944–6 N Spaulding
Avenue
Chicago, IL 60651
Tel: 312 227 1959

Gold Leaf Conservation
Studios
PO Box 50516
Washington DC 20004
Tel: 202 638 4660

Haas Wood & Ivory
Works Inc
64 Clementina
San Francisco, CA 94105
Tel: 415 421 8273

Hosek Manufacturing
Co Inc
4877 National Western
Drive, Suite 205
Denver, CO 80216
Tel: 303 298 7010

Mark A. Knudsen
1100 East County
Line Road
Des Moines, IA 50320
Tel: 515 285 6112

Albert Lachin & Associates
618 Piety Street
New Orleans, LA 70117
Tel: 504 948 3533

Mad River Woodworks
PO Box 163
Arcata, CA 95521
Tel: 707 826 0629

Maurer & Shepherd
Joyners Inc
122 Naubuc Avenue
Glastonbury, CT 06033
Tel: 203 633–2383

Mendocino Millwork
Hallelujah Redwood
Products Box 669
Mendocino, CA 95460
Tel: 707 937 4410

Nomanco Inc
Hershey Drive
Ansonia, CT 06401
Tel: 203 736 9231

W.F. Norman Corporation
PO Box 32
214–32 N Cedar Street
Nevada, MO 64772–0323
Tel: 800 641 4038

Nostalgia Architectural
Antiques
307 Stiles Avenue
Savannah, GA 31401
Tel: 912 232 2324

Old World Molding &
Finishing Inc
115 Allen Boulevard
Farmingdale, NY 11735
Tel: 516 293 1789

Royal American
Wallcraft, Inc
Crown House
834 South US 1
Fort Pierce, FL 33450

Sheppard Millwork
21020 70th Avenue West
Edmonds, WA 98020
Tel: 206 771 4645

Silverton Mill Works
Box 850–FAA
Silverton, CO 81433
Tel: 303 387 5716

W.P. Stephens Lumber Co
145 Church Street
Marietta, GA 30061
Tel: 404 428 1531

Tiresias Inc
PO Box 1864
Orangeburg, SC 29116–1864
Tel: 803 534 8478

Vintage Wood Works
513 S Adams Dept 704
Fredericksburg, TX 78624
Tel: 512 997 9513

Walker's
PO Box 309
Tallmadge, OH 44278
Tel: 216 633 1081

J.P. Weaver Company
2301 West Victory
Boulevard
Burbank, CA 91506
Tel: 818 841 5700

PAINTS & STAINS

Evergreene Painting
Studios Inc
365 West 36 Street
New York, NY 10018
Tel: 212 239 1322

Gold Leaf Conservation
Studios
PO Box 50156
Washington DC 20004
Tel: 202 638 4660

Martin Senour Company
1370 Ontario Avenue NW
Cleveland, OH 44133
Tel: 216 566 3140

Benjamin Moore & Co
Chestnut Ridge Road
Montvale, NJ 07645
Tel: 201 573 9600

The Old Fashioned Milk
Paint Company
Box 222
Croton, MA 01450
Tel: 617 448 6336

Pratt & Lambert
Box 22, Dept GV
756 Tonawanda Street
Buffalo, NY 14240

Rust & Co
2105 Payne Street
Alexandria, VA 22314
Tel: 703 836 6010

Wold Paints And
Wallpapers
771 Ninth Ave (at 52nd St)
New York, NY 10019
Tel: 212 245 7777